Troubled Pilgrimage

Passage to Pakistan

Balwant Bhaneja

TSAR

We acknowledge the support of the Canada Council for the Arts for our publishing program. We also acknowledge support from the Government of Ontario through the Ontario Arts Council.

We acknowledge the financial support of the Government of Canada through the Canada Book Fund for our publishing activities.

Canada Council for the Arts Conseil des Arts du Canada ONTARIO ARTS COUNCIL CONSEIL DES ARTS DE L'ONTARIO Canada

Cover design by Ingrid Paulson
Cover photo by Stuart Hughes
Journey map by Joám Evans Pim

Bhaneja, Balwant, 1941-, author
Troubled pilgrimage : a passage to Pakistan / Balwant Bhaneja.

Includes bibliographical references.
ISBN 978-1-927494-26-4 (pbk.)

1. Bhaneja, Balwant, 1941 – Travel – Pakistan. 2. Diplomats – Travel – Pakistan. 3. Diplomats – Canada. 4. Pakistan – Description and travel. I. Title.

DS377.B53 2013 915.49104'53 C2013-904565-1

Printed and bound in Canada by Coach House Printing

TSAR Publications
P. O. Box 6996, Station A
Toronto, Ontario M5W 1X7
Canada

www.tsarbooks.com

For Alexander and William

Contents

Islamabad
3
Lahore
2/7
Indus
River
Shikarpur
5
Sukkur
4
Rohri
6
1/8
New Delhi
PAKISTAN
Karachi
INDIA

1

Preface: Partition and Refugees

It was from New Delhi that I began my journey to Sindh. It was also from New Delhi, four decades earlier, that I had left for Europe, from where I would proceed to my future home, in Canada. Searching for our roots comes to us either in our youth as we try to shape our identity as distinct from that of our parents, or much later when we realize that our core self cannot be separated from the culture and heritage in which we were born.

The first time I became aware of Sindh, or those who came from there, the Sindhis, was one September morning as a six-year-old when I saw a group of dishevelled people with my father approaching our home in New Delhi. My father had gone to the Old Delhi Railway Station to pick them up as they arrived from Sindh. Walking slowly towards our ground-floor government quarters in Lodhi Colony, the stragglers included my silver-haired grandmother, Ammi, leaning heavily on my father's arm; the others were my father's eldest brother, an older cousin, two widowed sisters, and their families. Old and young, in all there were around fifteen people.

Carrying their meagre belongings in small tin trunks, tiny bedrolls on their heads, unkempt in unchanged clothing, they looked tired and forlorn. This was my family, who had come from the other side of the border, from the newly formed country of Pakistan, partitioned from British India on 15 August, 1947.

My father, thirty-one years old then, was a junior officer in British India with a secure government job in the Central Public Works Department (CPWD). Just before Partition he was transferred from Bombay to the central office in Delhi as Office Superintendent, one of the youngest persons so promoted, according to my eldest uncle Devidas. It was he, through connections, who had managed to get my father his first job in Sindh civil service after his matriculation.

Our four-roomed government quarter in Lodhi Colony had overnight turned into a refugee camp. My father helped to find jobs and shelter one by one for each of his siblings and their families. Over more than a year, my mother coped with this influx of relatives in addition to minding her own family of four. My grandmother stayed with us until her death at eighty-three. The joint family used to be the norm in those days, everyone pitched in to share the burden of household chores.

A civil service neighbourhood like ours in Lodhi Colony had people from communities from all over India. Parents would refer to the other children as "the son of that Bengali," or "that child of the Madrasi," and so on. Some Hindu and Muslim names come to mind from those childhood days—Dinesh, Radha, Suraiya, Kan-dama, Kasim. We are playing on green lawn late one summer evening, the children sit in a circle. One child gets up and runs around the circle with a scarf hidden under her shirt. As she runs, she quietly drops the scarf behind someone. We all sing—*Kokla chapake jumme raat ayi je, jehra aage pichhe dekhe, usdi shamat aayi je* (Kokla chapake it's Thursday night, anyone looking here or there is sure to be punished). The one who is unaware of the scarf dropped behind him is the loser.

But after 15 August kokla was not played again on that lawn. One morning we found that the families of Suraiya and Kasim had quietly disappeared during the night. Rumours were that they had gone into hiding in the Karbala ruins of Aliganj, to the west of our neighbourhood. From there, they were to be escorted by their people or the police to Pakistan. The following afternoon we saw a mob break into their homes, taking away whatever they could. This happened just before the arrival of my relatives from Sindh, who brought similar stories with them.

I came to realize that my father and his people belonged to a community who were from a distant place on the other side. A sense of religious communal consciousness began to shape my mind, where the others were Muslims and my folks who came from Sindh were Hindus. I learned that unlike refugees from Punjab in the west and Bengal in the east, the Hindu Sindhis had no land mass of their own in the new India. In that, my newly arrived relatives fitted the classic definition of a "refugee"—the homeless, without earth and hearth of their own.

In this company of new arrivals, and the people who came to visit our home, the names of Indian Independence leaders such as Jawaharlal Nehru, Mahatma Gandhi, and Sardar Patel permeated the discussions. I was too young to understand politics, but there was great admiration for these leaders and their vision of a free India. Of the three, it was Mahatma Gandhi whose name was most frequently mentioned, either in admiration for having achieved freedom for India, or in anger for his failure to avert Partition. Despite the massacres and the displacement that followed the unexpected division of India, it was Gandhi whose aged, fragile voice on the radio every evening gave hope and solace. Communal riots between the Hindu and Muslim communities were a frequent phenomenon on the subcontinent. But usually, after a season of arson and riots, the two sides having exhausted their vengeful emotions would calm down, and life would return to normal.

Between October and December that year I recall on two occasions taking my refugee relatives through the lush Lodhi Gardens to Birla House to get a glimpse of Mahatma Gandhi at his prayer meetings. My father's office in those days was near the Central Secretariat complex, and on those afternoons he would come south from his work to meet us at the gates of Birla House. He seemed to have great trust in my sense of direction as a six-year-old.

Birla House was a large two-storied colonial building, lime washed in bluish white, owned by the industrialist G D Birla. Gandhiji's prayer meetings were held on the wide lawn at the back of the spacious building and were open to the public. It is only now that I realize the impact those two visits to Birla House had on me. Somewhere in my life's journey, as he had been to millions around the world, Gandhi would become my ideal, affirming that amidst unchecked greed and violence it was human to be ethical.

Now I was once again in Delhi, on the eve of my departure to Sindh, my ancestral homeland. With continued hostilities between the two neighbours, mainly over the disputed region of Kashmir, the hope of travelling to the other side for my parents' generations had gone unfulfilled. I had noticed a similar aching wait during the Cold War among my Canadian friends from Eastern Europe, who had given up on ever being able to visit their homelands. In the case of my family's homeland it turned out to be a different story—standing for decades on an imaginary border between India and Pakistan, they grew old; eventually death cheated them of their hopes.

It is amazing how most of us wish to die in our own land—the notion of one's land has that sense of comfort, a profound sense of security even at death. It is in our homeland that our past lives and our memories linger forever. I felt my dead parents' spirits rekindling in my bones an intense desire to make the pilgrimage across the border to their home towns in the Upper Sindh. I had another link with Pakistan. It was in Lahore, the capital city of Punjab where my father was posted from 1939 to 1942, that I was born.

Two days before my planned departure for Pakistan, Dr Savita Singh, Director of Gandhi Smirti Foundation in Delhi, suggested I visit Birla House. Memories from my childhood flashed through my mind. The road on which Birla House stands has been renamed Tees January Marg, commemorating the date of Gandhi's assassination, the 30 January, 1948.

Sindhu Kala Kendra under the Patronage of Shri Sugumal Bhaneja Presented TABLEAU showing Shri Uderolal classical Sindhi style on Republic day, the 26th Jan. 1960.

2

Gandhi Darshan in Birla House

On his last birthday, two months after Independence, a despondent Mahatma Gandhi replied to a friend: "Send me condolences, not congratulations"—referring to the bloodbath the partition of the country would bring, and the continual antagonism that would follow.

Of all the times I had been in Delhi since I left India, only now did I feel a strong desire to revisit Birla House. It was Gandhi who said that following the principle of ahimsa (nonviolence) in search of Truth was not something for an extraordinary person; anyone with self-discipline and the desire to be ethical could achieve it. Over the years I had sought to understand the meaning of that Truth. The search for Truth through nonviolence is not something unique to India and its ancient Vedic scriptures, these core values are common to all the world's great religions. It depends on the interpretation and practice of received teachings. Truth is revealed when one is ready for it.

When on January 30, 1948 Gandhi was killed by a Hindu Brahmin, instead of riots breaking out the country went numb. The nation was in a state of shock. I wonder what would have happened had Gandhi's assassin been a person from the Muslim, Christian, Sikh, or Dalit community instead of a Hindu. Perhaps that would have resulted in communal killings similar to those in Delhi in 1984 when, following Prime Minister Indira Gandhi's assassination by a Sikh bodyguard, thousands of innocent Sikh families, mainly poor and working-class living in Delhi's shanty towns, were massacred by political mobs. Similarly, communal riots in Gujarat in 2002 were directed at thousands of labour-class Muslim families in state-supported killings by Hindu fanatics.

On the days following the assassination of Mahatma Gandhi, all shops and offices in our neighbourhood were closed. There was almost no traffic on the streets. A sense of profound sadness hung over everything. One of the songs released then, becoming popular overnight, related the martyrdom of the "Father of the Nation." Sung by the renowned Mohammed Rafi, the song—*Suno, suno yeh duniya walon, Bapu ki yeh amar kahani / woh Bapu jo pujya hai jitna Ganga ma paani* (Listen O people of the world, the immortal story of that father sacred as the waters of Holy Ganges)—when played on radio even today it brings back clearly the memory of those sad days.

Unlike other Gandhi Memorial Museums I had visited across India, Birla House stood out for its unparalleled historical significance. The museum focuses on the 144 days, from September 9, 1947 to January 30, 1948, that Gandhi spent at the house.

Standing on the lawns, I looked back at the house, at

the room with the high French doors. A six-year-old holding on to my father, I recall, I watched in the evening light Mahatma Gandhi slowly stepping out from that room. Everyone is hushed in anticipation of the great man coming down the path. Wearing a white dhoti and a plain cotton shawl to protect his bare chest from the winter evening, a scrawny sombre man in round wiry glasses walks gently, his head slightly bowed, resting his arms on the shoulders of two young women in white (his great-nieces). They come towards the prayer dais, which is covered by a white sheet. A small coterie of men and women sit on the dais. As the old man sits down, the service begins with devotional songs.

The singing was followed by a short discourse by Gandhi. All India Radio broadcast Gandhi's prayer message every evening. In these discourses, Gandhi spoke about the need for compassion, forgiveness, and self-control, beseeching his listeners for intercommunal harmony. There were massacres taking place across the provinces of Punjab, Uttar Pradesh, and Bengal, and in Delhi itself.

Holding on to my father's hand, listening to Gandhiji on the white prayer dais six decades ago . . . Bapu, Daddy, and I were here. Now, standing in the same spot I felt a lump rising in my throat.

> I shall work for an India in which the poorest shall feel that it is their country, in whose making they have an effective voice; an India in which there shall be no high class and low class of people; an India in which all communities shall live together in perfect harmony. There

> can be no room in such India for the curse of untouchability or the curse of intoxicating drinks and drugs. Women will enjoy the same rights as men. We shall be at peace with all the rest of the world. This is the India of my dreams.

That bold vision remains to be convincingly articulated by any other Indian political leader. The corner room on the ground floor where Gandhi spent most of his time looks the same as on the day of his assassination. It has Bapu's meagre possessions: reading glasses, a walking stick, a knife, a fork, a spoon, and a stone that he used as soap for his bath. Gandhi needed only a white bedsheet spread on the ground on a thin duree mattress, a white gaddi cushion to sit, a low wooden desk to place papers for reading and writing, and a pillow by the wall. Whether in a large mansion or in a sweepers' colony, these were his humble belongings.

It was in this room that Gandhi undertook, on January 13, 1948, his last fast. Undertaking fasts was part of his Satyagraha (Insistence on Truth) and the most potent nonviolent weapon he used to atone any wrongdoings he may have committed or for the misdeeds of others. He went on such fasts to stop the violence that resulted from Hindu-Muslim discord, the persecution of the casteless poor, and against the unfair treatment of political prisoners during the Independence struggle. He had learnt about abstaining from food and water from his mother, who in his childhood would undertake fasts to pray for forgiveness of sins. This fast, which would turn out to be his last, he said he would break only when the city of Delhi showed a change of heart and genuinely embraced the victimized minority of Muslims with love.

A Gandhi biographer, Geoffrey Ashe, describing this period, writes that in spite of his old age Gandhi's adamant attitude in not breaking his fast until the zealots of both the Hindu and the Muslim communities gave their promise to stop the violence was addressed to the consciences of all, in both India and Pakistan. Gandhi "summoned them to pause and reflect. If Hindus, Muslims and Sikhs recovered their sanity; if even one of the three communities did so; if Pakistan became truly pak (pure) . . . then (he) would go his way in light and peace" (Ashe, p 378).

Bapu's footsteps are replicated in stone, going down the path until they abruptly end as he met his assassin's folded hand in the Indian greeting of namaste. That spot is marked by a column. It stands on a black marble platform, under a red stone canopy held by four slim round columns, and carries an inscription consisting of Gandhi's last words "Oh, God" in Hindi and English on two sides, with the date and time of his death.

He Ram,
5:17 Evening,
30.1.1948.

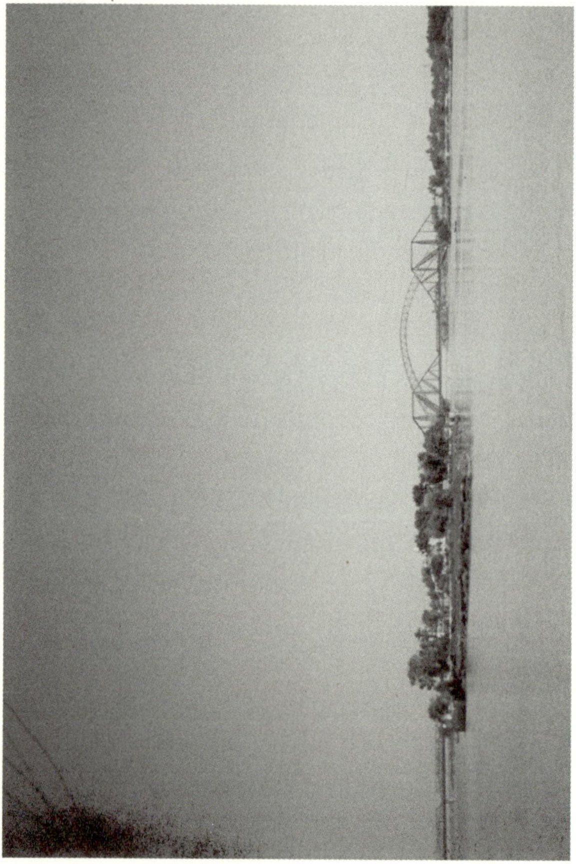

3

On the Way to Ancestral Lands

The Indus is a long river, starting high up north in Mansarovar Lake on the Himalayan plateau in Tibet and cutting through Pakistan from Kashmir through Punjab to Sindh, before emptying into the Arabian Sea. Its ancient name is Sindhu and the people who lived by its banks are Sindhis. Sindh is one of the two largest provinces of Pakistan, its capital the port city of Karachi on the Arabian Sea.

As a child I would hear from my refugee relatives their nostalgic stories about this legendary river, the Muslim and Hindu Sufi saints and fakirs who lived by its banks, its folklore, and the poetry and festivals celebrated on its shores. It was strange that these new arrivals, while talking about communal tensions between Hindus and Muslims, in the same breath would use the Hindu name Bhagwan and the Muslim name Allah for God. They praised endlessly the poetry of the Muslim Sufi poets. Even the word for mother in Sindhi used by Hindus and Muslims of that generation was the same—Ammi.

In 2005, Sindhis in Pakistan comprised 12 percent of its populace, in total 30 million people, while the dominant linguistic group, the Punjabis, consisted of 48 percent of the country's 165 million. Pakistan is an Islamic state with 96 percent of its population Muslim and the remainder 4 percent Christian, Hindu, and Sikh. Sindhi Hindus form a tiny portion of the overall population of Pakistan, less than 1 percent.

My parents were born in Upper Sindh, north of Larkana, of families that came from the small towns on the banks of the Indus. My father was born in Rohiri on its east bank, and my mother in nearby Shikarpur on the west bank.

Stuart Hughes, a friend from my diplomatic days who was posted in Islamabad as Deputy High Commissioner, had warmly responded to my idea for this trip. On hearing about my intent to venture into these towns rarely travelled by foreign tourists, he had done some research for my travel. He advised that to start the journey in the capital, Islamabad, would be fitting as it would provide me with a good overview of modern Pakistan. The twin cities of Islamabad and Rawalpindi were worth visiting, as well as Taxila, an hour's drive to the northwest. This was the oldest route to the subcontinent, used since the times of Alexander the Great by invading armies on their march through Afghanistan to India (and during the British Raj in the opposite direction).

There was a modern highway between Islamabad and Lahore, but the road between Lahore and Sukkur—my first destination in Sindh—was described as unsafe. The itinerary for my Sindh-Punjab journey that Stuart chalked out was to fly into Lahore from Delhi and on to Islamabad, from where I would take a local flight to Sukkur. For my return trip from Sukkur, he suggested I take the overnight train from Rohiri Railway Junction to Lahore. From Lahore I would fly back to Delhi. It all sounded reasonable. I had little choice in making my travel plans as I had no one from my parents' time in those Upper Sindh towns to advise me.

Compared to the congested Indian airports, Lahore's Allama Iqbal International Airport and the two regional airports I passed through, newly constructed and spacious, were relatively empty. While waiting for my flight to Islamabad, a local English newspaper left on a chair in the lounge caught my attention. It had on its cover page a colour photograph with the headline: "Holi celebrations in Lahore." The photograph showed Muslim and Hindu friends and their families gathering on the occasion of the Hindu festival of Holi, smearing red and green gulal powder on each other's cheeks. When you have lived all your life across the border (or as far away as Canada), thinking of the two communities in terms of stereotypes hating each other, this picture of warmth and hospitality in a leading Pakistani newspaper came as a shock and wonderful surprise. Just a few hours before on the other side of the border in New Delhi, celebrating the same annual Hindu festival at my cousin's house, no one could have dreamt that similar celebrations were going on in Lahore. Even if one had thought of such a possibility, the event in Lahore making the front page with a colour photo would have astounded everyone.

Another of my Pakistani stereotypes was broken when as an Indian-born Hindu I was effortlessly checked through Customs and Immigration at the airport. During immigration clearance, I was dreading a rough interrogation by stern "enemy" officials with thick moustaches such as those depicted in Bollywood thrillers. Instead, at all the three immigration control booths, the officers turned out to be cheerful women in smart Punjabi dress uniform, without hijabs, who courteously checked my documents and questioned me politely.

In my travels, rightly or wrongly, I would use the status of women as an indicator of Pakistan's modernity. This was perhaps a result of the post 9/11 stereotypes acquired in the West. I was quickly processed to the departure lounge for my Islamabad flight. It was silly of me to have felt uneasy. Security services have better things to worry about than shadowing a middle-aged tourist. Our stereotypes are shaped by the daily dose of information from television and newspapers. The usual festive Holi mood across northern India that year, according to TV channels in Delhi earlier that morning, was sombre. This was attributed to the bomb blasts in the religious city of Varanasi a week ago, which had taken the lives of twenty-one innocent people in a busy market square. A Muslim Kashmiri terrorist group had claimed responsibility for the killings.

The desire to visit Sindh had arisen many years ago on my father's seventieth birthday, when he was visiting me and my family in Bonn, Germany, where I was posted as a Canadian Foreign Service Officer at the Embassy during 1983–87. It was during a stroll along the Rhine that he had mentioned how the river reminded him of his home town of Rohiri. Every time he visited us in Bonn, he would frequent the river, and watch its flow and admire the backdrop of the Siebengebirge hills. The seven hills formed a shape like a slumbering dragon. I doubt if there were any similarities between the waters of the Rhine and the Indus, except their north-south direction, which might have taken my father back to the days of his childhood. The Rhine, however, flows in the opposite direction, from south to north, and drains into the North Sea. It happens to be one the busiest waterways of Europe, freight-carrying barges plying it in both directions day and night. The nonstop traffic of barges, the dance of light and shadow on the flowing river beat to the rhythm of human life.

During my four years in Bonn, my father visited every year, breaking his journey to India to come see Neil and Raoul, his two grandchildren. He had multiple homes now, including his own in New Delhi, where my mother had decided to stay with my youngest brother Harish, and the one in Ottawa where my other brother Suresh and sister Damayanti lived. Just as in his early years in Delhi, on his arrival in Ottawa he became involved in the resettlement of new immigrants. The move to Canada was triggered by a heart attack he had suffered some years before. We had all felt that living in Canada would be therapeutic for his health, allowing him to take his mind away from the hectic family and social pace of Delhi. However, those who are accustomed to being busy get busy wherever they are. He seemed perfectly content with his gypsy-like arrangement which he described as having homes on three different continents.

This time when he came to visit us, I suggested that he stay on longer and spend his special birthday with us in Bonn. To mark this occasion my birthday gift to him was a father-son trip over the long weekend to a destination of his choice. He chose London, as he had never been to the UK before.

That Easter weekend we flew into Heathrow from Cologne, checking into a modest hotel in central London near the British Museum. During that visit, I noticed that he was reading a book entitled *The Sindh Story*, by K R Malkani, which a friend from India had sent him. He was impressed with this rare contemporary history of Sindh and suggested that I read it after he had finished it.

On Sunday we sat in the Georgian park beside a cherry tree near our hotel on Tavistock Square. To our amazement, there was a larger-than-life bronze statue of a sitting Mahatma Gandhi, a shawl draped round his bare shoulder, in the middle of the park in the midst of bright yellow tulips in full bloom. Gandhi with his eyes closed, his head bowed, and deep furrows of age and burden on his forehead, was in a contemplative pose that we had never seen in a Gandhi statue anywhere else. It was a gift from the Indian High Commissioner in the UK to the City of London.

We imagined young Gandhi in this neighbourhood in the 1880s, a law student walking to the nearby

Temple Inn to attend his classes. The neighbourhood is filled with rows of Victorian regency houses, some of the homes with small blue plaques bearing names of famous people who had lived there. It is interesting that despite the acrimony between India and Britain at the time, none of the freedom fighters—Gandhi, Nehru, or Mohammad Ali Jinnah—had shown any hatred for England or the English; instead in their writings they describe fond memories and affection for its people and the land.

As we sat in the Tavistock Square park, I suggested to my father that it would be wonderful to do a similar father-son trip to Sindh in the near future; this time we would reverse our roles—he would be the guide and show me the places where our family came from, where he was born and went to school, where he and my mother got married. "Perhaps, some day," he replied wistfully. Four decades after the Partition, political tensions between India and Pakistan continued—the creation of Bangladesh and wars over Kashmir had left deep wounds in the psyches of the two nations. The time was not right, my father said. We both knew that a visit to Sindh was not a practical suggestion. I had naively thought that if this father and son trip to London could happen in our lifetime, visiting the land of my ancestors could someday be equally possible.

One evening we attended a play in the West End. My father was a playwright and had a love of music. In Delhi he was always active in organizing cultural events, most of them for raising funds for refugees of the Partition. I sat through many rehearsals late evenings in various homes and usually ended up cast in small roles as a refugee child in his social dramas, a street urchin helping the family by selling newspapers or shining shoes. My father's two notable plays, *Sharanarthi* (Refugees) and *Aage Badho* (March Ahead), were performed under the banner of Our Arts Society in 1949 and 1950 in Delhi's then stylish Regal Theatre in Connaught Place.

The play in the West End in London was called *The Orphans,* with Albert Finney as the lead. It was set in New Jersey, with only three characters, two delinquent brothers living in dilapidated quarters and an older man, Finney, whom they accidentally kidnap. It was the kind of theatre my father liked, with societal overtones. He found the youths' alienation in the play depressing. One of his favourite works happened to be Thornton Wilder's *Our Town.* A drama critic of the *Statesman* in Delhi, while reviewing *Aage Badho,* had recommended that the young playwright, because of his interest in social realism, read Wilder for inspiration. I am not sure to what extent my father pursued that suggestion, but by the early nineteen sixties he was working on larger cultural projects focused on propagating Sindh and its culture in India.

We returned to Bonn, my father telling everyone how wonderful his seventieth birthday treat had been. A few days later he flew back to Canada. That was the last time I saw him. Two months later he passed away in Ottawa, of heart failure, far from the Indus of his birth.

Our identity evolves in peculiar ways. It is only near the end that we come to terms with what and where we were destined to be. I was born in colonial India, became a part of a wider refugee community in independent India, and then at twenty-three left as a young engineer to work as an apprentice for an architect in Hamburg, Germany. The idea was to see the world and to advance my education. When I left home in the spring of 1965, I never thought that instead of returning to India I would end up in Canada—that I would give up the safe profession of civil engineering and enrol instead to study journalism and international relations, ending up in the field of science policy to become the first South Asian science diplomat in the Canadian Foreign Service. As a struggling student I met an Irish girl called Marie from Dublin, fell in love with her, and had the courage to propose and to marry her.

Looking back, I could see I was never one for safe choices. The parochial surroundings in which I grew up were those where one's identity was defined not by who you were but by whose child you were, the caste you belonged to, the city or village you came from, and the language you spoke. These were your introduction cards for acceptance or dismissal regardless of your intellect or competence. Departing for Europe first and then for North America was exhilarating. It made me feel for the first time culture-free, gave me a sense of freedom from the lumbering tradition around me. At twenty-three, however, such a feeling of confinement and a desire to jump out from the narrow circles of conventions is natural, regardless of culture or country.

My parents, especially my father, were generous in letting me, and their other children who came after me, leave home, confident that this would better our futures. Perhaps the fact that they themselves had to leave their homes when young explains their comfort at letting us go.

Having finished my foreign service career, one afternoon while browsing through my bookshelves at home in Ottawa I happened to come across the book, *The Sindh Story,* which my father had been reading twenty years before during his visit to Bonn. As I flipped through its pages, I saw the neatly written comments in the margins made by him in pencil. Busy at work and home raising a young family, I had never had the chance to read it. Perhaps I knew of the strong improbability of ever visiting Pakistan or Sindh. Even though the writing in pencil had faded, there was something striking in the way my father wrote his *S*'s and *I*'s. The desire to visit the other side, Sindh—the land of my ancestors, resurfaced.

I would have to make this journey alone. With the passing away of my parents' generation, I had no way of knowing about possible friends or relations in Sindh. When it came to national stereotypes on either side of the border, things had not changed much since the Partition. Pakistanis continued to see Indians as large bullying neighbours, whereas the Indians saw Pakistanis as fanatics always ready to encourage and harbour terrorists against India. This was further complicated by the insularity of the sizeable Muslim minority in India and the tiny Hindu minority in Pakistan. The general perception within my Hindu Sindhi community was that due to the migration and ethnic cleansing of Hindus in Pakistan during Partition, there were hardly any Hindu Sindhis left there.

4

Islamabad: An Abode of Islam in a Modern Capital

Quaid-E-Azam Airport is marked as Point Zero—south of it is the old garrison city of Rawalpindi, to the north lies Pakistan's capital, Islamabad, established in 1962. Both cities share the airport. My flight from Lahore arrived late in the evening at the QEA. I was dazzled by the bright lights outside. As Stuart was busy with a Canadian delegation, he had sent his driver to pick me up. Smartly dressed in blue jeans and a short jacket over a check shirt, Ronnie was in his mid-twenties. A Christian Pakistani, he spoke good English, and he would be my driver and guide for the next few days in Islamabad.

Driving out of the airport in the dark of night, we turned left towards the nation's capital into a six-lane boulevard. The brightly lit high-rises flanking both sides of the road made me think we could be driving through a European capital. Noticing my appreciation, Ronnie remarked that one of the best highways in the country was the newly built four-lane motorway on which one could drive to Lahore in less than five hours. Ronnie had not been to Canada, but those whom he had taken to Lahore had remarked on the similarity to a Canadian highway.

We were passing by a mound on top of which stood a lit-up, larger-than-life portrait of a solemn-looking man, two-to-three-storey high, wearing a triangular hat. The portrait's outline was shaped by a blue neon light. The figure was that of Pakistan's founding father, Mohammad Ali Jinnah, benevolently gazing down at the traffic. A large board bathed in bright floodlights below the figure proclaimed "Faith, Unity, and Discipline" as the values of Quaid-E-Azam (The People's Leader).

Jinnah's vision of Pakistan as a republic, with Islam as the declared state religion (in contrast to India's secular constitution), was that of an inclusive and pluralist democracy with equal rights for all its citizens irrespective of their religion, caste, or creed. In his famous speech as the first President of Pakistan's Constituent Assembly, he described his vision of Pakistan as follows:

> Now, if we want to make this great State of Pakistan happy and prosperous we should wholly and solely concentrate on the well-being of the people, and especially of the masses and the poor . . .
>
> You are free; you are free to go to your temples, you are free to go to your mosques or to any other place of worship in this State of Pakistan . . . You may belong to any religion or caste or creed—that has nothing to do with the business of the State . . . in course of time Hindus would cease to be Hindus and Muslims would cease to

> be Muslims, not in the religious sense, because that is the personal faith of each individual, but in the political sense as citizens of the State. [Stanley Wolpert, *Jinnah of Pakistan*, pp 339-40]

Coincidentally, that declaration in many ways is similar to the speeches given by Indian leaders of the time. Pakistan's founding father was also in fact a refugee. He was born in the Gujarat province of India, where Mahatma Gandhi also hailed from. Jinnah's vision of unity among the diverse ethnic and religious groups that had emerged in Pakistan eroded rapidly after his death, a year after Pakistan's independence.

Suffering from weak lungs, and a heavy smoker, Jinnah died at the age seventy-two, seven months after Gandhi, in 1948. With the predominantly military rule that followed, initiated by General Ayub Khan and succeeded by the more orthodox General Zia-ul-Haq, Pakistan's Constitution was written and rewritten subservient to Sharia laws based on the teachings of Islam. While I was looking at the giant neon figure, Ronnie declared, "We are on Mohammad Ali Jinnah Avenue, the main road into the capital."

The destruction of the World Trade Center on September 11, 2001 in New York and the subsequent regime change in Afghanistan had created a new security environment on the subcontinent. Taliban and Lashkar-e-Taiba, which previously had free reign in the north, from Afghanistan to Kashmir, as non-state actors, were now officially regarded as terrorists. Pakistan's President General Musharraf had been the target of these terrorists' bombs, narrowly escaping attempts on his life. Some of these incidents had happened in Islamabad, which from a security point of view was supposed to be the safest city in Pakistan compared to the crowded Peshawar, Rawalpindi, and Karachi.

In this new security environment, one noticed the evidence of a thaw in bilateral India-Pakistan relations. The heads of states of the two countries had recently exchanged visits. In 2004 the Indian prime minister Atal Bihari Vajpayee had invited Pakistani president Musharraf to visit India. It was a bold initiative, as Vajpayee's Bhartiya Janata Party (BJP) was regarded in Pakistan and by many in India as a Hindu-chauvinist party with an inflexible position on the disputed issue of Kashmir. A year later Musharraf followed up on Vajpayee's invitation and made an unprecedented visit to India to commence a "composite" dialogue process.

Soon after, the BJP opposition leader and its president L K Advani, a Karachi-born Sindhi, went on a visit to Sindh. In his speeches delivered in Karachi at public meetings the BJP leader was now talking about the ongoing peace process between India and Pakistan as irreversible, and seemed convinced that there were solutions to all the issues between India and Pakistan including that of Kashmir. There was a feeling in the air that things were changing for the better between the two neighbours.

As he lived by himself, Stuart had invited me to stay with him. Unlike most diplomat families that resided in compounds, Stuart's home was outside, in one of the well-developed Sectors of Islamabad. He lived in a two-storey semidetached house with a small lawn in front. Knowing that part of my visit to India was linked to meetings with peace researchers and civil society groups, Stuart asked if I would be interested in attending a public meeting on the Land Mines Ban Treaty he had organized for a Canadian delegation next morning. I thought this would be a good opportunity to learn about the treaty and to visit the Quaid-E-Azam National University.

On our way to the university in the morning, we drove through the official centre of Islamabad, populated with well landscaped modern city blocks and office buildings. We were again on Jinnah Avenue, which ends in front of a building called Eiwan-E-Sadar, the official residence of the President. President Musharraf used this building primarily for meetings with foreign dignitaries; his residential quarters remained in the adjacent city of Rawalpindi, which had been the location of Pakistan's armed forces headquarters since its creation. As we turned right to the adjoining Constitution Avenue, a row of modern monumental buildings appeared on large tracts of properties: the National Parliament, the Supreme Court, and the Prime Minister's Secretariat.

Comparing Islamabad's architecture to that of India's capital, the two cities very obviously represented the contrasting national visions of their respective countries. While New Delhi's official buildings, designed by Sir Edwin Lutyens, combine an eclectic mix of Hindu, Mogul, Roman, and Victorian architectures executed in pink and red stone, the planners of Pakistan's capital had focused on specific Islamic architectural perspectives, modern but austere, utilizing elegant, clean geometric lines in whites and greys to create grand designs that framed concrete in attractive monumental blocks.

Islamabad in Urdu means the "Abode of Islam." All offices were moved from Rawalpindi in the 1980s after the completion of the new city. The capital's imposing setting has Margalla Hills as a background in the north, merging with the Hindukush Mountains in the west. In the East, beyond the mountain resort of Murree, they extend into the Himalayan ranges.

Pakistani Peacekeepers and Land Mines Ban Treaty Seminar

Quaid-E-Azam University is situated north of Constitution Avenue, near Murree Road close to the hills, with a view of Rawal Lake in the distance. It was established in 1967 as the University of Islamabad. A decade later, aspiring to be a national university, its name was changed to honour Pakistan's founding leader. The university looked like any other campus with male and female students in small groups strolling outside or sitting in the shade under leafy trees in the campus grounds.

The Land Mines Ban Treaty seminar there gave me an interesting perspective on the concerns of Pakistanis, the students in particular. Pakistan, they said, should not sign the treaty if India did not do likewise, and they were concerned about the more friendly attitude of the United States towards India. I learned that Canada now ranked 51 as a provider of the United Nations Blue Helmet peacekeepers whereas that year Pakistan ranked among the top ten suppliers. Canada had moved away from its Pearsonian peacemaking tradition post 9/11 and chosen to go into a war-fighting mode.

That afternoon Ronnie drove me to Margalla Hills. It was a clear sunny day. From the hilltop, in the far distance I could see Islamabad's key landmarks: the Saudi Mosque and its shining tall, slim, minarets surrounding a large white tentlike structure; Rawal Lake, which supplied the water for Islamabad and Rawalpindi; and the cluster of monumental buildings in the centre that I had passed by on Constitution Avenue that morning. The capital had an interesting layout—a triangular master plan based on a grid system, with blocks and sub-blocks, its apex reaching towards Margalla Hills. A large share of Islamabad city planning is credited to the Greek urban planner Constantinus Dexiadis. Dexiadis divided the city into sectors and subsectors cushioned by green belts and parks. The city reminded me of Chandigarh, the newly built capital of Punjab in India, designed by the French architect Le Corbusier. Ronnie said that the view of the capital from the Margalla Hills at night was spectacular.

As the wages were low in Pakistan, Stuart was able to hire Ronnie on an as-needed basis. Ronnie was recommended to Stuart by one of his Catholic relatives, who worked at the High Commission. Unlike other minorities, many Christians at the time of Partition chose to be in Pakistan, remaining or moving there from India, in the belief that Islam as a faith of the Abrahamic tradition would be more tolerant of Christianity.

Sufi Singer Abida Parveen—a Surprise Introduction to Sindh

I had a small package with me from Mumbai, given by my Indian ghazal singer-friend Mahesh Chander for the Pakistani Sufi musician Abida Parveen. Though Abida Parveen was from Sindh, she had homes in both Karachi (the capital of Sindh province) and Islamabad. She was recently widowed, and in her mourning she had taken to singing even more intensely her Sufi devotional repertoire.

The word "Sufi" has many associations. It has been linked with the Greek word "Sophia," a seeker of wisdom and truth. In Sindhi, the word "safa" means "pure," symbolizing purity of heart. The focus of the Sufis has been not on external appearance but on the call of unconditional love that emanates from one's spirit. Abida Parveen's renderings of Sufi and other poets such as Shah Abdul Latif, Buley Shah, Kabir, Farid, and Sachal have become known all over the world to those who know the language and its mystical poetry. She has a unique, unrestrained voice that lifts the yearning for spiritual love to its finest rendering. The Sufi poets, of independent mind and spirit, were traditionally poor mendicants whose belongings consisted simply of a coarse gown and an empty bowl, and a one-string Ektara instrument, which they carried as accompaniment when they sang or danced.

Mahesh's letter was to serve as an introduction, providing me an opportunity to make a courtesy call at this famous Sindhi singer's house. The package also had a CD with Mahesh's own recent compositions. When I called Abida's home, her brother Ali picked up the phone and informed me that Abidaji was out of town. She had gone to Bhit to sing at the mazar (shrine) of the poet Shah Abdul Latif on his anniversary. I was aware of Shah Latif's poetry since childhood, having heard my father and his two friends Dewan and Kan Motihar recite it in the most haunting voices. Ali told me Abida would be at the Bhit celebration for a week.

I was disappointed. I told Ali that as I was going later that morning to Taxila, I would send Mahesh's package the following day with the driver. Ali insisted, however, that as their house in West Islamabad was on the way to the ancient city, I must stop by to visit.

Ronnie drove me west through various sectors of Islamabad, past rows of large attractive bungalows and elegant houses. Abida's brother Ali was waiting for me at the gate of the house in the front courtyard. In his early fifties, he had an open face that stuck out of his dark turtleneck pullover. He wore western flannel trousers. Greeting me warmly, he invited me inside to describe to him what had brought me to Pakistan. It was cool inside the newly built bungalow. Ali pushed two cane chairs close to the outside wall so that we could enjoy the bright wintry sun filtering through the window.

Hearing about my plan to visit Sindh, he was delighted. "You must go there." When I expressed my concern about the safety of journeying alone in Sindh, he quickly remarked that there was nothing to fear about travelling in Sindh. "Sai, you would love it there.

They are very hospitable people. There is no difference between Muslims and Hindus in Sindh. It was never there." Was he saying that the violence in Sindh during the Partition period was not as vicious as in Punjab?

I recalled the stories I had heard from my elders about the bloodshed in the Lahore-Amritsar sector during the Partition riots. The burning of houses, the slaughter of trainloads of men, women and children, the deadly attacks on caravans crossing the border—those horror stories of the murder, bloodshed, abductions, and rape of women, and the separation of families had become legends in households on both sides. The estimated number of deaths ranges from half a million to a million. The magnitude of the horror should put any Indian or Pakistani to shame.

Ali said that unlike Punjab, Sindh during that period was relatively calm. Muslim neighbours implored their Hindu friends not to leave. When the Hindu families felt that they must, in case things got out of control, they did so under the protection of their Muslim neighbours. Hindu friends were escorted to the port city of Karachi and put on ships bound for Mumbai or on the trains for Rajputana (now Rajasthan). I imagine that my refugee relatives must have come by train to Delhi, crossing the border through the desert of Rajputana.

It is said that the riots that took place in Sindh were mainly in the southern cities of Karachi and Hyderabad, led by newly arrived refugee Muslims from India who were penniless and squatted on the properties of Hindus, reciprocating what was happening to theirs in India. Mr Khuro, Premier of Sind, wanted Hindu Sindhis to stay in Pakistan for their business acumen and modern education; they had the entrepreneurial skills and assets that a new nation needed. Defending the Hindus and their properties from being looted, he is said to have gone out in the streets in Karachi with a revolver in his hand (Malkani p 127).

When Gandhi's emissary, Malkani, requested permission from Premier Khuro in 1948 to tour Sindh in order to check out the conditions of the Hindus of Sindh, Khuro refused, asserting that Sindh could look after its own citizens, Muslims and Hindus. The new prime minister of Pakistan, Liaquat Ali, who was himself a refugee from India, however, found this pro-Hindu Sindhi attitude of the Sindh premier unacceptable, which resulted in Khuro's dismissal.

Ali mentioned that even today, in cities like Larkana, there was a large number of Hindus living side by side with Muslims. "Look at our language, food, music, culture—do you see any difference between Hindus and Muslims? We are like brothers." There was a genuine feeling in Ali's voice. "At places of Hindu and Sikh worship, even today we Muslims get invited to sing in praise of God. So don't worry. In Sindh, they will take you in their lap, and not let you go." I was amused by his Sindhi metaphor of "hanja mein," making me feel like a little child in a lap.

Ali did not know that in Sindh I would be going only to Sukkur, Shikarpur, and Rohiri, the places of my ancestral connections. I mentioned to him that my father had once said that the name Bhaneja meant "of Bhane." "Yes, yes," Ali replied, "there is still a village near Sukkur called Bhone." I wanted to ask him for a contact, but hesitated. Let the chips fall where they may, I told myself.

As I got up to leave, Ali remembered, "Near Taxila, there is a place that you must visit. It is the Sikh shrine of Panja Sahib. A great Sikh shrine with a lot of positive vibrations; you will like it there." Ali must have known of the great affinity the Hindu Sindhis have for the Sikh faith and its holy book and Gurus.

It is said that Guru Nanak Sahib during his wide-ranging travels visited Shikarpur, my mother's hometown, to spread his message of the primacy of formless Nama and Shabda, the Name and the Word, for seeking eternal Truth. The Sikh religion is a product of Sufi and Bhakti schools of thought, and its main holy book, the Guru Granth Sahib, comprises of select passages from various faiths and traditions, mainly Hindu and Muslim. During Sikh rule in the eighteenth century, the Sikh teachers who came to Sindh brought the Udasin tradition of worship and adoration, focussed on their holy book and the kirtan, the singing of sacred names, instead of worshipping idols as in popular Hinduism.

In fact, in Sindhi familial ceremonies such as weddings and funerals, even today one sees blessings sought from both Hindu temples and Sikh gurudwaras. At the first anniversary of my father's death, my mother, instead of Hindu Brahmin rituals, had decided to go for a Sikh memorial service involving a patth ceremony at our home in Delhi. It included two days of nonstop recitation from the Granth Sahib, and concluded with the serving of food to the community.

Ali went into the adjoining room and brought back a handful of Sindhi CDs and audio cassettes of Abida and gave them to me. Then remembering something, he rushed inside again. This time he had in his hands a woven cotton traditional ajrak chaddar (large shawl). I was struck by its colours and design—squares and floral weavings in earthy tones of vivid red, indigo, and mustard. Handing it to me, he said that it was a special present from him. "A blessed piece of cloth given to the family by a dervish, a devotee of Lal Sai of Sindh, who used to give such chaddars as blessings to their dervish followers. This is a memento of the trip to your parents' homeland." Sufi dervishes were essentially contemplatives while Sufi fakirs sang; however, both sought internal freedom and communion with the spirit. I was moved by Ali's generosity, in giving such a personal gift to someone whom he had met for the first time.

He came out to the gate to instruct the driver about the whereabouts of Panja Sahib. I asked Ali to pay my respects to "Adi" Abida. I was sorry to have missed her, but glad to have chosen to stop by at her home to meet her brother. It was years since I had used the word "Adi." In colloquial Sindhi "Adi" is used to address an older sister.

5

The Ancient Highway to Peshawar

I had not had the faintest notion that the Sikh shrine of Panja Sahib was located near Islamabad. Stuart had never heard about it either. I would have missed it if Ali had not mentioned it. This journey would keep throwing unexpected surprises my way.

Departing Abida Parveen's house around noon, we drove on to the busy old Grand Trunk (GT) Road that runs west towards Peshawar. Taxila is situated on this highway, from where the GT Road goes into the North West Passage of Karakoram and the famous Khyber Pass into Afghanistan. Outside Islamabad, we were now passing through small towns and villages. The small homes, unlike the big bungalows we had seen in Islamabad, were made of rough mud brick and mortar, without any plaster to cover them. The GT Road had heavy traffic, mainly trucks with large decorated canopies over the driver's compartment, painted with swirling psychedelic designs in bright gaudy yellow, red, and green. The canopies jutted out like colourful crowns on the front of the vehicles over the driver's seat. For local passenger transport, I would note throughout my travel, the three-wheeler autorickshaws had replaced the horse and donkey carriages. In this part of the country, it was now a six-passenger seater called "Quinghay," driven by bearded men on heavy Royal Enfield motorcycles.

The soil was rocky, and unlike Islamabad the mountains in the background were jagged and treeless. In bright sunshine and dry weather, the crumbling rocks produced a hue of beige dust blown by gusty winds. Ronnie decided that as Panja Sahib was beyond Taxila, he would first take me to the Buddhist-Gandhara museum, which was a must for tourists, and then drive me to the Sikh shrine.

The entire region around Taxila is steeped in antiquity. The ancient city dates back to 500 BC. Along with Peshawar, Taxila was a city of the Gandhara Empire that lasted from the sixth century BC to the eleventh century AD. Sculptures and archaeological digs show strong Greek influence, due to Alexander the Great's invasion in 334 BC. Subsequently the territory was taken over by Kushan and Maurya Kings and became a centre of Hindu and Buddhist learning. Taxila attracted students from as far as Greece and China and is the world's first university. The renowned Sanskrit grammarian, Panini, and the great teacher of statecraft, Kautilya, are said to be the products of this ancient university.

To go to Panja Sahib we had to return to the main road and travel another twenty kilometres. Panja Sahib is off the road, located in a tiny town called Hasam Abdal.

Turning right from the main road, we drove through narrow lanes, Ronnie reading signs in Urdu that pointed to our destination. Under the Urdu signs, there were directions also in Gurmukhi, the Sikh script. In the olden days, until the 1920s, my mother's childhood days, the main written language taught to Hindu girls in Upper Sindh was Gurmukhi (the language which came out of the mouths of the Sikh Gurus). This was to enable them to read scriptures and teach them to their children. Apart from that, learning to read was not deemed essential for girls who were trained by the older women of the family to be good wives and mothers.

I had heard a lot about the three prominent Sikh shrines on the Pakistan side of the border—Nankasahib (the birth place of Guru Nanak), Mardana Sahib, and Panja Sahib. In addition to his knowledge of Hinduism, Guru Nanak (1464–1539 AD) was greatly influenced by Muslim mystics like Kabir and Farid.

The story about the establishment of Panja Sahib as told by the local guide went as follows. Some people from the region went to Guru Nanak Sahib with a plea to protect them from a drought. Guru Nanak is said to have walked to a hillock and, standing before it, he pointed his staff at it and proclaimed that there was water beneath the rock. As Nanak tapped the boulder with his staff, the rock moved and rolled down, releasing the water underneath. With his "Panja" (his palm) Guru Sahib stopped the boulder. The rock still has the imprint of the palm, and stands amidst the gushing water that fills the pond surrounding the temple.

The number of people in the temple at that time of the day was not large. There was a two-storey-high security gate of wood with brass knobs and a smaller gate cut in one of the two panels to control the flow of people into the premises. The arch-shaped gate fitted well into the mouth of the wall, and seemed as if it had been built for an elephant to pass through. The security officials routinely checked the whereabouts of the visitors. This happened at all Sikh and Hindu shrines in Pakistan in order to protect them. Only Sikhs and Hindus were allowed inside. Once my passport was checked and my name confirmed that I was a Hindu, I was escorted inside to pay homage at the shrine.

It was quiet in the compound, with hardly twenty persons present. Covering my head with a handkerchief as per tradition, I washed my hands and feet in the fresh waters of the pond before entering the building. The cold, white marble relaxed my entire body, tired after walking about the archaeological digs at the museum in Taxila. The main hall had a large dome at the sanctum sanctorum, its ornate arched walls and ceilings decorated with a mosaic of small mirrors, and in this sublime splendour, at its centre, was the holy book, Guru Granth Sahib. There was a Sikh priest with a stringy beard and white turban reading the Book on the dais. A couple of microphones were laid around for devotional kirtan performed every morning and evening. I could imagine the Sikh devotional hymns echoing inside the hall. In India and Pakistan the Gurudwaras are more than a place of worship. In addition to enshrining the Granth Sahib, the temple serves as school, meeting place, and rest house for passing pilgrims.

Returning to Islamabad on that ancient highway I was reminded of the time in the past when I had longed to come this way. It was in the summer of 1967 during my road trip from Canada to India. Having hitchhiked in Europe, then travelled by local buses from Istanbul to Kandahar via Tehran, I had finally reached Kabul. Arriving in the Afghan capital, I found that Indian nationals, because of the recent war between India and Pakistan, were refused visas by the Pakistan Embassy. The goal of passing through the land of my birth through the Khyber Pass on this same Grand Trunk Road had to be abandoned.

In pre-Partition days, Mahatma Gandhi had met the nonviolent Pashtun leader Khan Abdul Gaffar Khan on this same highway near Taxila in the 1930s. The friendship and ferocity of Pushtuns, also called Pathans, are well known in the region. Ronnie explained that Pathans live by a tribal code of honour and loyalty. This code has to be protected at all costs, which often leads to violent tribal feuds and futile killings. The honour is enforced through the principle of revenge, based on the dictum "eye for an eye, tooth for a tooth." The British incursion into the North West Frontier tribal lands and the arbitrary demarcation of Afghanistan and British India by the Durand Line raised Pashtun fury many times in the nineteenth century. However, in this multi-generational battle against the British Empire, Abdul Gaffar Khan chose to oppose his brethren's ancient style of violent resistance.

Despite coming from a rich family of landowners, Khan Gaffar Khan in his youth had taken on the job of a village school master to teach the Islamic values of peace and charity. He became a staunch follower of Gandhi. Popularly known as the "Frontier Gandhi," Gaffar Khan also advocated nonviolent civil disobedience. I wondered if the origins of the well-known Gandhi maxim that, "eye for an eye only makes one blind," was a Gandhian response to the North West Frontier mind-set of "eye for an eye, tooth for a tooth." When the British proposed the division of the subcontinent along religious lines, Gandhi and Gaffar Khan were the two leaders who walked out from the Congress Party discussions. Choosing to remain nonpartisan on the eve of Partition, both men committed themselves to work on both sides of the border to bring inter-communal harmony. Gaffar Khan settled in Peshawar to seek Pushtun autonomy within Pakistan through nonviolent means. One of the most memorable photographs of Mahatma Gandhi is the one with this rugged, bearded, tall Pashtun leader in hand-spun kurta-pyjama walking with the diminutive bare-chested Indian leader in dhoti.

Gandhi was assassinated in India less than a year after the Partition, and Abdul Gaffar Khan, for his struggle for the autonomy of Northwest Frontier, spent most of his life imprisoned by the military rulers of Pakistan. He died in 1972 in Peshawar at the age of ninety-two. According to his wishes, he was buried in a border village in Afghanistan, close to Peshawar.

The Sikh priest in the Gurudwara had given me some dry powdery parshad made of suji flour to take home. I put the offering carefully in my knapsack to share it with some of my relatives in Delhi and Ottawa.

As we reached Islamabad, it had gotten dark. I was hungry and asked Ronnie to drive us to a good eatery for a bite. To our delight we found a Pizza Hut restaurant in one of the Islamabad sector markets. While breaking bread, we mused over our long day and the places we had seen. I took the opportunity to ask him about his wife and children and the plans for the next morning.

On my last evening in Islamabad, Ronnie drove me to the Main Railway Station in Rawalpindi. I had to purchase the train ticket for my return journey from Rohiri to Lahore. There were only three flights a week to Lahore from Sukkur, and there was no other way to return except to take the overnight train from nearby Rohiri. Earlier in the day I was told that it was unheard of western tourists using trains to travel in Pakistan. This was due not to security concerns, but to frequent derailments. Most accidents were caused by the poor conditions of the old rail tracks. In the first nine months of 2004 there had been sixty-three such derailments reported. However, these statistics did not deter me from buying my ticket for the journey from Rohiri to Lahore.

As we drove through Rawalpindi's dimly lit smog-ridden streets, I asked Ronnie about our whereabouts. He informed me that we were in the city's military cantonment district, and that the fortress-like building on our right was the Central Jail. It was here on the orders of military dictator General Zia-ul-Haq that the deposed prime minister Zulfiquar Ali Bhutto was hanged in 1979 early one morning.

Mr Bhutto, originating from an established Sindhi Muslim feudal family, father of former prime minister Benazir Bhutto (who was assassinated in 2007 on her return from exile), hailed from Larkana, Sindh. He was the founder of the Pakistan Peoples Party (PPP). A former foreign minister in General Ayub Khan's Government, with a stint as president (1971–73), and then as prime minister (1973–77), Mr Bhutto in a contentious trial was accused of authorizing the murder of a political opponent, and was subsequently hanged. The hanging of a democratically elected prime minister had stunned the subcontinent.

Twenty-six years later, it seemed that public opinion in Pakistan on the decision of the execution was still divided. Many, especially those from Bhutto's party, regarded him as a martyr executed for political reasons. The military rulers had felt threatened by Bhutto's broad political base.

On our way back to Islamabad, I had seen a sign for a university, this one named Shaheed (martyr) Zulfiqar Ali Bhutto Institute of Science and Technology (SZABIST). Its existence in the capital, now run by a military dictatorship, where he was hanged by a military government, seemed a bit bizarre. SZABIST, which officially retains the status of a chartered institute, has branches in Karachi, Larkana, and Dubai. I was curious what Ronnie thought about Bhutto's execution. His reply was that it had all happened long before his time.

I have always enjoyed the aerial views from the windows of a small plane. As we flew south from Islamabad to Sukkur, the propeller aircraft glided along a river. It was a clear sunny afternoon. I could see down below the thin curvy river, flanked by dry beds on either side, that gave one the sense of its width when in full flow. The snow in the distant mountains had not melted yet. On my side of the window, in the east, the terrain gradually began to change. The green fields shrank into small plots of land, merging into a vast ocean shimmering under the golden rays of a bright sun. I soon realized that I was seeing an optical illusion. The brilliance of the afternoon rays on the sand dunes over the eastern horizon had created from the desert a wavy ocean. The vast desert stretching across Rajasthan formed a natural border between the two countries.

Sindh is the southernmost province of Pakistan, with Karachi on the Arabian Sea as its capital. It covers an area of fifty-four thousand square miles. The only time I briefly visited the places of my grandparents in Upper Sindh was when I was five. This was to attend the wedding of my oldest cousin and the funeral of my maternal grandfather. Events come in interesting pairs. That trip from my childhood though vague is still etched in my memory.

Years ago I tried to recreate that journey in a short story, "Under the Starry Sky," published in *Manushi.* It was a tribute to my mother and an effort at trying to understand my relationship with her. The story explores the geography in my mind without my ever having been to Sindh, and is patched together with fuzzy memories of that childhood pre-Partition visit to

Rohiri, Sukkur, Shikarpur, and Lahore over half a century ago. This time I was on a real journey, navigating the gulf between imagination and reality.

The pilot announced in Urdu that in ten minutes we would be landing in Sukkur. The name is pronounced Sukhur with the emphasis on *kh*. As the aircraft taxied down the single runway, I noticed a relatively green cluster of tall palm and date trees on the west of the Indus. The small newly built airport, painted in a faint yellow wash, gleamed in the afternoon. In my parents' time, Sukkur did not have an airport. This one was part of the government's plan to develop Sukkur as the northern Upper Sindh regional hub for economic development. Even though it had only three flights a week to Lahore, it had daily connections with Sindh's capital and Pakistan's largest port city of Karachi.

6

By Daryah Indus in Sukkur

There is a well-known boat song that all Sindhis know, *Jhuley Jhuley, Jhuley Jhuley Lal—aseen nimaana aiban wara* (O Jhuley Lal, bless us we frail humble folk). Jhuley Lal, a mystic, is also known by other names, Udero Lal, Amar Lal, and Lal Sai. It is said that during the rule of a local tyrant in olden times, the persecuted people of the kingdom stood on the banks of the Sindhu and prayed to the god of the river for a saviour.

Holding my brown duffle bag in my hand and with green knapsack on my shoulders, at Sukkur airport I looked for the information counter or a phone link for local hotels. The two hotel names for Sukkur given to me in Islamabad were Inter Pak and Forum Inn. They were provided with the caveat that they would be like a two-star motel. A security guard, at the airport information desk that I located, confirmed their existence. He saw the look of a lost stranger in my face and told me to wait and sent one of his assistants to get me a taxi.

The assistant returned with a tall man in baggy shalwar trousers and long shirt. He had a weathered complexion and a thick moustache. When I mentioned the two hotels suggested to me in Islamabad, he said both were equally good. I wondered if he was just being tactful. Forum Inn was in the centre of town close to the main market; Inter Pak was quieter, near the daryah, the river. He took the duffle bag from me and put it on his side seat as I climbed into the back of the taxi.

As we drove out of the airport he curiously asked me if this was my first visit to Sukkur. He seemed to be having difficulty placing me regionally. I understood my parents' language well, but it was rusty. Though I spoke Sindhi hesitatingly, it was understandable. I had tried it in Islamabad with Ali and thought it sounded fine. However, I did not know the regional origins of my dialect. Since I had learnt it from my parents, I assumed it came from here, the region of their birthplace. Having grown up largely in Hindi—and Punjabi—speaking neighbourhoods in Delhi, I had picked up those two languages at school and on the street. At home our parents spoke in Sindhi while we replied in Hindi. Conversing with the driver I was surprised to discover that Sindhi words that I had not heard since my childhood now came easily to my lips.

He asked if I was a medical rep touring the area. I kept quiet. I was not sure whether to tell him where I came from or about the purpose of my visit. In the post 9/11 climate, one had to be cautious whether in New York or Sukkur. Upper Sindh had a reputation for robberies and kidnappings. I remembered newspaper stories of innocent Indians held in Pakistani jails for years, having been arrested on charges of spying. Similar stories were reported of Pakistani jasoos (spies) caught in Old Delhi's Muslim areas. I had decided that on this trip I would try to avoid being drawn into any political talk. Even the camera I carried with me was a cheap disposable one, in case my expensive Canon be confiscated by the authorities. When I had expressed this concern to Stuart in Islamabad, he had assured me that unlike most Canadians, in Pakistan I had the unique advantage of being an invisible minority. We had both laughed at the thought.

The driver recommended Hotel Inter Pak. I went with his choice; he assured me that I would be pleased with its location. The Inter Pak was at the city's landmark, Sukkur Barrage. He asked me if I would need a taxi tomorrow; I ignored his question, asking instead about the barrage. The dam, built in the years 1923–34 across the Indus River by British engineers, stood as a solid masonry wall of yellow stone, the waters of the river controlled by large wooden sluice gates. There are sixty-six sluice gates on the mile-long barrage.

When we drew up at the hotel, the driver again asked about my plans for tomorrow. He wanted to know if he could come to pick me up in the morning. He was keen not to lose the fare. His taxi was a grey rusty Toyota, a 1986 banger without air-conditioning, and I was not sure if I wanted to spend the day simmering in it. There was little choice however and the six hundred rupees fare for the day was dirt cheap. The man looked honest. I named the three towns I intended to visit—Shikarpur, Sukkur, and Rohiri. He said he would show me all three for an additional four hundred rupees, promising to be at the hotel at nine in the morning. It seemed a reasonable arrangement. I asked him his name. Grinning, he replied, "Nur Bux."

Hotel Inter Pak turned out to be as Nur Bux had described. It was situated on the west side of the river between the two canals that ran westward in the direction of Larkana and Dadu. It was a relatively new two-storied red brick building with some forty rooms and a narrow lobby. The rooms were of motel quality—rundown by overuse, narrow, and dimly lit. The hotel was used mainly by travelling officials from the district and tourists on their way to the Mohenjo-Daro archaeological site, a three-hour excursion from Sukkur.

The site, linked to the five-thousand-year-old Indus Valley civilization, was discovered as a well-developed city; the one unusual aspect of the city was that no weaponry was found in its excavation. Hence the theory that it was not destroyed by a war but perhaps by a natural calamity. One proposal is that an unexpected shumal, a desert storm, buried the city overnight while its citizens were asleep. Mohenjo-Daro in Sindhi means the Mound of the Dead.

The room, though poorly painted, had a large bed with clean sheets, an attached bathroom, and a colour television; it looked comfortable enough to spend the night in. I turned on the television. I had been watching the Sindhi KTN channel for the past few days in Islamabad, using it as a window into my parents' culture. It was fascinating for me to see daily news, political debates, and sports, music, and drama coverage all in Sindhi. There is very little broadcasting in Sindhi in

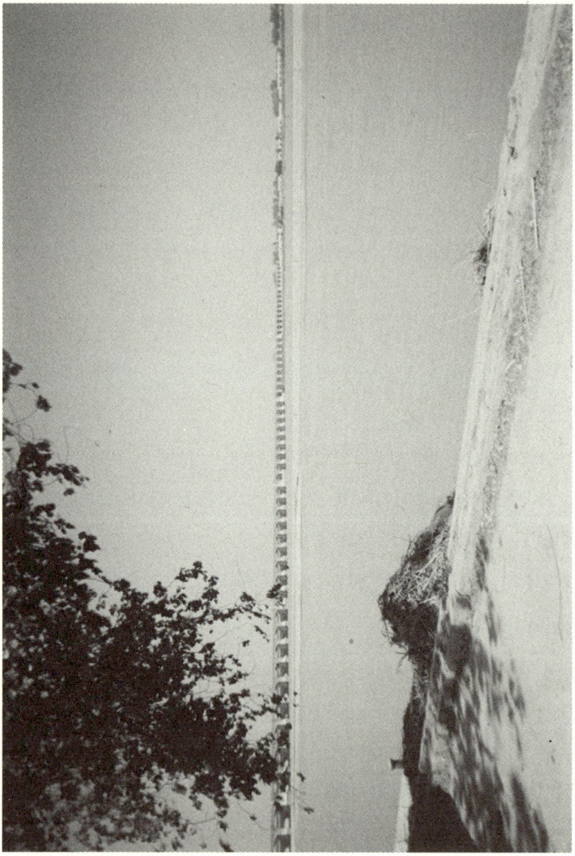

India. In the presentation of Sindhi programs here, one saw a sense of confidence in the language spoken and the varied expressions that must come from it having its roots firmly in native soil. The population of Sindh is around thirty million, whereas the Sindhi population in India is estimated to be just three to four million.

In India, in the absence of a land mass and despite the best efforts of the government and local communities to preserve the Sindhi language, I heard all my life predictions of the eventual demise of our mother tongue. That early enthusiasm together with various state initiatives for preserving Sindhi had begun to wane in India. The language did not have the same appeal to children born in India as it did to their parents who had grown up on this side of the border.

A feeling of deep satisfaction surged through me at having put my feet on the soil where my ancestors were born, my mother in Shikarpur, my father in Rohiri, and my aunts and cousins in Sukkur. This was the land they had longed to see again. A Lahore-born Indian, who had lived his childhood and youth in India, and settled in faraway Canada, I was a rare species even among my own; and it was I, of all my large family, who had come back to our land six decades after the Partition.

There was enough time before sunset, so I decided to step outside and take a walk by the barrage at the hotel gate.

The view of the massive wall spanning the gently flowing Sindhu in the shadows of the late evening was enchanting. One of the three canals that passed by the hotel was called Dadu Canal. It was in the southern town of Dadu in the district of Sewan that my father had landed his first job. My uncle Devidas, sixteen years older than my father, was the head of the family, my grandfather having died when my father was six. My uncle, a tall man with an authoritarian demeanour, was an imposing personality. He was the one who talked about the customs and rituals of biradari to be maintained when it came to the important events of life. I imagined how he must have instructed my father to be proper and respectful while taking him to Dadu to introduce him to his contact in the local Public Works Department. Even with regards to my parents' arranged marriage, in addition to my widowed grandmother Ammi, he would have been the one involved in the negotiations, ensuring that the girl was strictly from the same community, well-mannered, and obedient, and the amount of dowry to be given by the girl's family was in line with the local community council's stipulations. Betrothals in those days took place with brides as young as fourteen.

There was no traffic except for a two-wheel horse carriage trotting on the side street along the river. I turned left towards a public park to get a closer view of the river.

A vendor at the park gate was selling peanuts from a cart. Smoke from his little round clay pot, which had burning coal inside, drifted upwards. The pot, placed over the peanuts, was to warm the shells. I bought a handful and the vendor wrapped them in a newspaper. The park was quiet, with a few men and women, and children playing with a ball. The scene was similar to ones in towns all across India. But here the language and dress were different. The dress worn by the women was local (not the burka), with a dupatta covering the head, like my mother used to wear, and a couple of men had donned a Sindhi topi, the colourful embroidered round cap with a small triangular slit in front.

I sat on a wooden bench closer to the water. In the long shadows of the evening the temperature was slowly cooling. There was a young couple sitting on a bench nearby. I wondered if they were lovers. Their informality suggested to me they were married. They glanced curiously at me, and then again quickly became engrossed in their conversation.

As I broke the peanut shells, I watched the river lazily roll by. I could see on the opposite bank, the town of Rohiri where my father was born and grew up to be a teenager.

The last rays of the sun made the houses in the distance take on the brilliant golden hue of the land. I imagined my father as a teenager playing with his friends, jumping in the water or walking home by the river, returning from school. Rohiri was known mainly as a railway junction where trains from Rawalpindi in the north and Karachi in the south stopped, while some branched off westwards to Larkana and Quetta. Otherwise Rohiri was just a small town adjacent to Sukkur, the centre of commerce.

Unlike Sukkur, with its business focus, Rohiri was a place with ordinary people—peasants, teachers, civil servants, and a couple of doctors. Besides its railway junction, it was known for its saints and mystics. The saying goes that in Rohiri under every stone you turned you found a Sufi saint. The town produced "sava lakh pirs and sants" (twenty-five thousand saints). I remembered from my childhood names of Hindu saints such as Paroo Shah, Vasan Shah, Baba Nebhraj, Sai Moolchand, and Dr Rochal Das, all from Rohiri. These holy men were known for their community services and for performing miracles that ranged from curing the sick to materializing amulet talismans and vibhuti ash from their palms. The devotees of these pirs and fakirs believed in instant recovery from deadly accidents and incurable diseases by the application of ash.

As I listened to the sluggish flow of the river I was reminded of Jhuley Lal, the Sindhis' most revered saint from ten centuries ago, believed to have emerged from these waters. At the altars in Hindu Sindhi homes and temples, on important occasions it was to Jhuley Lal that everyone prayed. A big man with a crowned head and flowing silver white beard, seated cross-legged on a large fish, was how he appeared from the river. Jhuley Lal's appearance had brought communal harmony. Muslims have the equivalent of Jhuley Lal in Lal Shabaz Qalandar, who lived in Sehwan in ancient times. He too is associated with the river. A popular folk song involves Jhuley Lal and Shabaz Qalandar, and goes, *O, Lal meri pat rakhiyo bhala Jhuley Lalan . . . dama dum Mast Qalandar . . .*

I felt elated at the memory of this song praising Jhuley Lal and Mast Qalandar, which I had heard throughout my childhood and youth. Hindu and Muslim singers like Runa Laila, Nusrat Fateh Ali Khan, Master Chander, Ram Panjwani, Abida Parveen, the Motihar brothers, Bhagwanti Navani, and Mahesh Chander have sung these devotions each in their own inimitable ways.

My father was fond of the mystics. He had once proposed a most unusaul project involving Jhuley Lal that was accepted by the Government of India as Delhi State's tableau for India's 26 January Republic Day Parade in 1960. It was a huge float with the saint appearing in his white flowing beard on his mount of Pallo fish. It consisted of two fish-shaped panels, forty feet long and eight feet high, mounted on truck sides and pulled by a tractor. The panels were painted in soft brown colours with silvery strokes, highlighting the Pallo's glimmering scales and fin. On top of the float, a small temple of the Hindu God Shiva had been built, with men and women singing and dancing in colourful traditional costumes.

This was the first time ever that Sindh, despite not having a land base of its own in Independent India, was represented at the national Republic Day parade. The float was recognized as one of the best in the procession that year. Prime Minister Jawaharlal Nehru later invited those who participated in the Jhuley Lal tableaux to his residence at Teen Murti for a reception. That photograph taken with the first prime minister was a matter of great pride for my father.

The Motihar brothers, who specialized in putting the poetry of the older Sindhi poets to music, had provided the musical component for that Republic Day float. The brothers hailed from Sukkur; both had the typical long faces with thin noses that my parents and others also had. The older brother, Kan, who was dark, had a great sense of musical composition. It was he who had arranged the music for many Sindhi projects, including one on Shah Abdul Latif's special anniversary for Delhi's Akashvani television program. The younger brother, Dewan, of a fair complexion unlike his brother, had a powerful voice that captured the essence of the grand meanings of Sufi lyrics.

In my father's writings and the Motihar songs lie the spirit of Sindh. The haunting voices of the brothers rendering songs of parting and union came back to me as I sat there. They, like my father, died in their seventies, their dreams to sing in Rohiri and Sukkur unfulfilled. They all played a great part in interesting me to write, and encouraging me to appreciate the culture of my origins.

It was getting dark and the park began to empty. The vendor with his cart of peanuts was packing up to leave. The experience of being raised on the bank of this river must impact deeply. Wistfully in the twilight by the Sindhu River I recalled memories that my elders had imparted to me. The women who at dusk came to float "jyoti" lamps, tiny cups made of flour with butter and a lit-up cotton wick, as an offering to Udero Lal; the tonga-trip across the barrage to Sukkur on Saturday evening, where the youths from Rohiri would go to see the bioscope—the talkies; the milkmen crossing on their inflated bags of goatskin to deliver milk every morning to residents on the other side of the river . . .

The reverence for the river was inbred in the community. I could see this in my mother. Whenever we travelled by train in India or abroad, my mother would have a fistful of uncooked rice to throw from the train when passing the old steel bridges, saying aloud: "Jhuley Lal!" Years later when I was posted in Bonn, my mother, after performing her husband's last rites in Ottawa, stopped off for a visit with us on her return to India. On a bright fall afternoon we had taken her out for a boat cruise on the Rhine. In midstream she took out from her purse a small amount of rice and threw it into the water, saying, "Jhuley Lal!"

There was little activity on the other side. Unlike during my parents' time, there were no women there to float jyoti lamps or perform evening arti prayers. I returned to the motel. It was a starlit evening; I could hear the sounds of crickets and the flowing water from the canals. In the small dining room there were only three of us, quietly eating our evening meal.

Back in my room, I lay down on the bed looking up at the ceiling where the green paint was peeling. I wondered about the towns I was to visit in the morning. How much should I reveal about myself to the taxi driver? My fears had not eased. There were too many "what ifs" to dismiss my concern for safety in this turbulent country. As far as the next day's program was concerned, there was not much to plan, since I had no idea of who I was seeking or where I was heading. There was hardly any tourist information in these small towns, not even a map. And as for people, it was only the spirits of my ancestors I knew of, no one else. The sounds of frogs and crickets and the gurgling water from the two canals lulled me to sleep.

In one of my diplomatic postings in Europe, a senior colleague, introducing me to a visiting friend, had lightly remarked, "You know, Bill (short for Balwant) has an interesting background." After describing my origins in India, he had added, "He lives in three worlds at the same time." The comment took me by surprise. It is interesting sometimes the way others observe you. I presumed by the three worlds he had meant Canada, where I had studied and was now settled down as a householder; the Celtic Ireland of my wife Marie; and the Partitioned Indian subcontinent where I was born.

I mused on these three worlds. After all my years of living abroad, I still had a deep affection for the Indian subcontinent. It wasn't just love for its dualistic and non-dualistic spirituality, or a craving for Bollywood movies, music, or spicy food. India was where I was born, grew up, and spent the years of my early youth. It was still my native land despite being partitioned. Longing for it and caring for the welfare of those who lived there was in the soul, whether its people happened to be from one side or the other side of the border. At the same time Marie's Irish heritage brought to me a deeper understanding of Christianity than I would have ever had, an understanding that defined *Christian* as an adjective. Then there was North America with its rampant individualism, where you could see people in their zeal to succeed (or survive), with unrestrained egos, hoping to become billionaires like Rockefeller, Bill Gates, and Donald Trump—wearing a halo that celebrated without guilt the characteristics of greed and selfishness. Yet one could see in these egotistical projections a sense of anxiety which drew many to their own faiths or to new ones, seeking answers to the complex problems we all lived with.

Over the years it had become easy for me to slip back and forth between these three worlds, feeling both at home and an outsider in all three. Belonging everywhere and yet nowhere might make you pragmatic and practical, but with so much self-absorption there was a risk of becoming emotionally arid. Perhaps that was a reason for this journey.

7

Shikarpur—My Mother's Town

Kinakhi ayan, kinakhi jaanan,
ishk allahey ahe cha,
viruhu allahey aahey cha.

(I am nothing, I know nothing,
would someone tell me what is love,
what is separation?)
—*Sachal Sarmast, eighteenth century Sindhi Sufi poet*

The sun was already high when I got up. It was quite early, almost three hours before the taxi man's expected arrival. I slid open the thin tinny patio door of my room to step out onto the cement porch for a quick look at the passing waters of the canal and the small cement block houses on the other side of the canal. The water was high, rapidly flowing westward. It was time to get ready for the day, which I knew was going to be a long one. I took a shower and got dressed and began to pack my duffle bag. The room attendant brought me breakfast on a wooden tray—two buttered toasts and tea in a kettle with a chipped spout. I had no idea what sort of lunch or dinner would be available on the road.

I switched on the television to look at the KTN channel, which I had come to enjoy. Morning news was followed by a program of popular music. A young woman sang a ballad I knew well, composed by the Sindhi poet-saint Bhagat Kanwar Ram. The singer was Renu Gidoomal whom I had heard in London many years ago.

Wearing dark slacks and top, with a guitar in hand, Renu was belting out *Kinya rijhaya tokhey, kinya parchaya* (How do I please you, how do I appease you, please tell me a way, my beloved Lord). It was a 1920s devotional song. From the look of the auditorium and her audience, it seemed I was watching a music video from London or elsewhere that KTN had in its collection.

At nine o'clock, the phone rang. The clerk at reception informed me that my driver had arrived. I told him to send the man to my room. When I opened the door Nur Bux, with his friendly face, was there in the same outfit I had seen him wearing last evening. Despite his dyed hair, the end of his drooping black moustache showed grey at its ends. He must be in his fifties. I invited him to sit down on the chair. Hesitating, he took the seat. The time had come to tell him about myself, where I came from, my local origins, and the reason for my visit. I would repeat the same story many times during the day as an introduction. He seemed quite struck by my connections with India, Canada, and Sindh. In any case, the answer to the question "Where do you come from?" as I have mentioned earlier, does not come easy to me. A factual reply might be, "A Canadian Hindu Sindhi of origins in pre-partitioned India, born in Punjab." This is the simplest formulation of my awkward identity.

I outlined to him landmarks that I could recall from my only visit to the region as a five-year-old, Lakhi Dar in Shikarpur, Sadh Belo in Sukkur, Chabutra and Sai Vasan Shah's shrine in Rohiri. These were the names I had collected by scraping my memory, and asking older cousins in Delhi and Mumbai. Would it be possible to cover all that in a day? I had a night train to catch at 10:30 from Rohiri Junction to Lahore. I wondered if these places existed or they were just a figment of my imagination. He nodded that those locations indeed existed. He saw no problem in being able to show me all the places and drop me off at the train station.

His suggestion was that we start with Shikarpur, as it was in the west and the closest to the hotel. Then he would bring me back to Sukkur and we would go through the city, both its old and new parts. After that he would take me to Rohiri. He did not seem to be sure about places in Rohiri, as the locales I mentioned were in the older part of town. He assured me, however, that we could ask around there for places and my family connections.

I checked out of the hotel. Nur Bux took my duffle bag and put it in the trunk of the car. I always carry my small green knapsack with me. It contained my plane tickets, notebook, map, a book or two, and a water bottle.

We were on our way to Shikarpur.

It was another bright sunny day in March, slightly cool but much warmer than it was in Islamabad. Nur

Bux said that it would get warmer during the day. The road followed the railway track in the westerly direction. We reached a fork, the driver stopping to check the traffic; one road went north to Jacobabad and Quetta, the other proceeded to Larkana in the southwest. In my readings on Sindh, I had come across the names of a broad range of Muslim and Hindu intellectuals and activists who hailed from Larkana. They were known for a movement called the "Sindhiyat," aimed at raising Sindhi consciousness and identity. Ibrahim Joyo, Sobho Gianchandani, G M Saiyeed, and Haider Bux Jatoi were some of the names, belonging mainly to poets and teachers, who had feared the loss of Sindhi identity due to the large influx of Urdu-speaking Muhajirs from India. These activists had been seeking the rightful status for Sindhi language and culture from the central government for years. Their claim was that Sindh had suffered because of the policies of "imposed homogeneity," which compelled all to adopt a standard form of Islam, and Urdu as the national language (spoken at the time of Partition by only 2 percent of its population). They took great pride in Sindhi as a two-thousand-year-old language with fifty-two letters (whereas Urdu was only three centuries old and evolved as a language on its own during Moghul rule in India. Urdu has only twenty-six letters). This policy of homogeneity imposed by successive central governments (mostly military rulers) had eroded their cultural heritage. The harshest comment I had read on this question was by G M Saiyeed, who had gone so far as to claim that it was ideologically impossible for Sufi Sindh and Islamic Pakistan to coexist. (Malkani p 138)

Shikarpur was situated on the Jacobabad railway line. In my imagination, the road to Shikarpur passed through a dried-out barren landscape, therefore the farms on both sides of the paved road took me by surprise. When I mentioned this to the driver, Nur Bux with a smile assured me that this part of Sindh had always been green, at least in his lifetime. Since Sukkur Barrage was built about eighty years ago, the whole region was well-irrigated through its extensive canal system and benefited from two harvests a year.

The rabi (spring) wheat bushels were at their full maturity, and when the rains came the ground would be furrowed, this time made ready for the kharif (autumn) crop of rice paddy. What else was grown here? "Everything—fruits, dates, and vegetables." These were the local staples and traded in Sukkur's wholesale markets for shipments to Karachi, Larkana, and other parts of Sindh.

For arid land and desert, he said, one had to go north of Shikarpur towards Jacobabad or north of Rohiri in the direction of Multan, where scorching hot weather in the summer made the soil dry. That area was well known for its cotton fields. I observed the scenery as we drove along. The road was lined with rows of stunted thorny keekar trees. Delhi's red rocky terrain, when it was less populated, used to have the same kind of trees. On both sides of the road, the wheat and bajra plants were swaying in a gentle breeze. We passed by several small sleepy hamlets with mud houses and shacks, typical of rural regions on the subcontinent. I asked Nur Bux about his family. He had three sons, one in the army, another in the navy, and the youngest still in school. He was happy with their careers and enjoyed driving the taxi despite the ups and downs of the business.

I was in a rapturous mood. I imagined for a moment my newly wed mother returning with my father and his family on this very road to Rohiri after their wedding. It must have been on two-wheel horse buggies in the 1930s that the wedding party trotted back from Shikarpur to Rohiri. My father had come from Karachi to get married. I imagined myself on the same road a few years later, a five-year-old accompanying my mother to her father's funeral in Shikarpur.

I asked the driver if he could read Sindhi. He said, "Certainly, Sai." I took out my father's book from my knapsack. As the driver's hands were fixed on the steering wheel, I showed him the book. It had on its cover a photograph of my late father in front of our Delhi house. Bux read the Sindhi title on the cover page—*Des-pardes* (This land, the other land). I was happy that he could read Sindhi. Pointing to my father's picture, I said, "That's my walid sahib." With some pride and emotion.

It must have been the air of Sindh that made me light-headed, wanting to recite an old Sindhi poem. I asked him if he had heard of the famous Sindhi poet Sachal. Keeping his eye on the steering wheel, he smiled. "Yes Sai, Sarmast Sachal, he is our famous Sufi poet." Sarmast was the alias of an eighteenth century poet and means "the intoxicated truth seeker." I asked him if he would mind joining me in a Sachal Sarmast poem I knew. He smiled, I sang as he hummed along,

Kinakhi ayan, kinakhi jaanan, Ishk allahey ahe cha, viruhu allahey aahey cha. I am nothing, I know nothing. Would someone tell me what is love, what is separation? When I finished, Bux smiled at me and said, "Sai, I did not know this one."

My eyes welled up for a moment at my spontaneous rendering of Sachal, and I sensed the presence of my parents around me. The song plays in my head when I think of Sindh, my father, and his two musician friends, the Motihar brothers. On special events at home marking a festival, my father would drag my mother to come and dance with him in the traditional Sindhi styles of Ho Jamalo and Chej. The beauty of Sindhi Sufi poetry, whether written by a Muslim or a Hindu, was that the poems were about love with a double meaning: the love for the beloved and God were the same. The final union with the beloved was a total surrender, eliminating distance between Thou and I. There was a moment of silence as Nur Bux drove me towards Shikarpur.

After we had been on the road for an hour, Nur Bux swerved the car to the left into a neighbourhood which he described as the outskirts of Shikarpur. He seemed to have already mapped out an itinerary for me. We stopped near an old haveli with high stone walls enclosing the property. There was a tall wooden gate with two flanks; a sentry in khaki uniform holding an old flintlock rifle sat lazily on a bench. Nur Bux said that the government had posted the guard for the security of Hindu worshippers, and I should show the guard my passport. Nur Bux explained to him that I was a Hindu. Then turning to me he informed me that we were at the largest Hindu temple of Shikarpur.

Nur Bux reassured me, "You will meet your people inside." He meant inside the temple. "They may be able to tell you all about your relatives from Shikarpur."

I entered the compound behind the large gate of the haveli. A middle-aged man in white pyjama and shirt welcomed me. He was one of the volunteers at the temple responsible for receiving visitors. After listening to my story that I had come from India and Canada, he introduced me to a couple of other worshippers and showed me around. He was from Jacobabad and visited this temple a couple of times a year. There was no such temple in Jacobabad.

There were clusters of small buildings inside the premises, which included two temples, one with the Sikh holy book, Granth Sahib, and the other with the idols and photographs of the Hindu gods Shiva, Rama, and Krishna, and several ancient and contemporary gurus such as Guru Nanak, Jhuley Lal, Dada Vaswani, Baba Nebhraj, Sathya Sai Baba, and Shirdi Baba. The variety of those being worshipped confirmed that there was little orthodoxy in worship here; one chose one's favourite god or guru for salvation, accepting all traditions as equally true. There were a couple of rooms on the premises for the out-of-town pilgrims to stay overnight.

It seemed that I had arrived during morning prayers, which were being held in the open courtyard. There was a guru with a white shawl draped over his shoulders.

Basking in the morning sun, he was sitting on a string charpoy, his eyes closed. He had a full head of grey hair and a couple of days' growth of beard. There was a gathering of thirty to forty people facing him, waiting to listen to his discourse.

The volunteer took me to the farthest corner inside the compound. He wanted to show me the temple's most ambitious project—a large gou-shalla (cowshed). The building under construction had bays planned for fifty cows, where the congregation intended to raise them to worship and to produce milk and dairy for the community and others who might want to buy. This was of significance, because Pakistanis were predominantly meat eaters who consumed beef on special occasions like Eid.

I was then shown to a modest guest room. There was a cotton durree spread on the ground. We sat down while someone brought tea in a glass tumbler and biscuits from the tiny communal kitchen next door. Having heard my reasons for travelling to Shikarpur, my volunteer guide called an elder who might be knowledgeable about local families from pre-Partition days. Shikarpur in those days, because of its location at the crossroads of Quetta and Larkana, was a centre of finance, known for its traditional hundi system of banking, where money transfers took place by shroff traders. I gave the elder the details I knew of my maternal grandfather. His name was Mukhi Chella Ram and the family profession was that of jeweller and goldsmith. The title "Mukhi" signified his social standing as the head of his clan. I tried out the names of my three maternal uncles—Girdhari, Manohar, and Bihari. After Partition they had chosen to stay on.

The bespectacled old man with a deeply wrinkled face looked through his thick lenses. 1945 was too distant for him. My maternal grandfather had died sixty years ago, and his children, if alive, would be in their eighties now. It seemed I was at least one generation late in coming back. I consoled myself that I had not come hoping to find my relations. But then there is always a glimmer of hope that something unexpected, an accidental meeting, might happen on such a trip.

The members of the congregation were hospitable. Both my driver and I took the tea and snack offered to us. As I was getting up to leave, the volunteer suggested that I should pay my respects to the guru of the temple. I did not want to disturb the congregation, but when the volunteer walked over to the guru, I quietly followed him. He whispered into the guru's ear. On the latter's approval, I approached the man respectfully. He looked at me carefully and put his hand on my head as a blessing. He then took a large piece of white poplin lying by his side and put it around my shoulders, saying that I should get a shirt made out of it on my return. I touched his feet in the traditional mark of respect and came out of the premises.

Back in the taxi, Nur Bux asked me if I was pleased with my visit to the temple. Indeed I was. I was delighted at this completely unexpected encounter with local Hindu Sindhis. Meeting anyone from my mother's family would have been a bonus. The gentleman inside the temple had mentioned that in Shikarpur there were four hundred to five hundred Hindu households while in his hometown of Jacobabad the number was almost double. This was news to me as I had imagined that due to the Partition there would hardly be any Hindu families left living in Sindh.

Shikarpur was a small town with narrow streets and a mix of new and old houses. There was a gritty macadam road that circled the town. Nur Bux drove towards a relatively crowded crossing, one of the paths leading into the congested bazaar where no vehicles were allowed. At the crossing there was a beige-coloured tower. It was the famous Lakhi Dar, which my mother and uncles had spoken of. "Dar" means a gate, but that was in the old days when the city was walled. It had a kilometre-long bazaar passing through it. In the old days there were four entrances to the walled city. Now there remained only Lakhi Dar, with no gate, no walls, only a tower. The thirty-foot or so high tower with a round clock on top was sheltered by a dome. The tower itself was painted pink and was of concrete. The marble foundation stone at the bottom had the names of two benefactors, Jai Ram Bajaj and Righi Ram Bajaj, from 1935. The commemorative plaque stated that this clock tower was constructed to honour the English governor of the time.

According to Nur Bux, the entire region of Sukkur, which comprised Shikarpur, Rohiri, and other small settlements, had a population of around ten lakhs (one million). At the other end of Lakhi Dar, the crowded bazaar ended in the Gol Market. As the taxi could not plough through the lane, I got out of the car and walked into the bazaar. It was covered by worn-out canopies of cloth, extending over the shops from both sides as protection against the sun. Underneath, like most old districts, the market was in dilapidated condition. It was somewhere here, I thought, that my mother's paternal home would have been. My maternal grandmother had died when my mother was barely seven. In the absence of a mother she had an unusual childhood. Unlike most girls, who in their early teens learn from their mothers' experiences how to run a household, she grew up playing out her early years here with her three older brothers. When she was married, I had heard stories from the elders about her ineptness as a new bride who could not sew, cook, or read. But by the time she had raised the four of us, she was known for her warm hospitality and the delicious food which she prepared herself.

Nur Bux said that Lakhi Dar was still known for its ice cream and stringy faluda. He showed me a small shabby building owned by a Hindu businessman. At that early hour of the day, I did not want to sample anything. We drove around the town, checking out a couple of houses and a school where my cousin's wife Rani had gone. I had no addresses, just approximate locations given to me, based on vague recollections of the distant past. Nur Bux went through some small streets, and then we turned towards Sukkur.

It had become very warm. As I sat in the back seat of the car, the breeze from the rolled-down windows brushed my face. I was thinking of my mother and her family. How far she had travelled in all those years—Shikarpur to Ottawa! All the places she had lived in with her husband as part of his transferable CPWD job: Karachi, Lahore, Bombay, Delhi, Nagpur, and for a couple of years Phuntsholing, Bhutan, where my father was posted for some years on deputation. Then after my father's retirement, even Germany and Canada. Her story was sad. In her old age she wanted to live in the family home in Delhi that my father had built, surrounded by her family. But all the children left one by one, even her husband—who loved to travel and went on to spend more time with the children and their families abroad. It was the story of her life to bear the pains of separation.

We hardly saw any of her family. Motherless, she had looked up to her big brothers. After Partition they were untraceable, lost. Every time my mother met someone who had come from Pakistan, she would inquire about her missing brothers. She never received a satisfactory answer. Some said that they had moved to Jacobabad after Partition and converted to Islam. Some said that the three men had become vagrants, involved in street fights and scuffles, on the run from the law. There were rumours that they were killed in the Hyderabad riots of 1948. Yet some consoled Mother by saying that her brothers were alive, but having converted to Islam they had changed their names. Having married Muslim women, they had severed connections with the local Hindu community. The truth was that if they were alive, they never made any effort to get in touch with their younger sister. Their fates unknown, her brothers were lost to her forever. As the taxi bumped along towards Sukkur, I stared blankly at the passing scenery.

8

Sukkur: Its Hindu Traders

The flickering light through the projection room widens into the larger-than-life images of hero and heroine of yesteryear, Karan Dewan and Suraiya, on the white screen. The round-faced heroine sings *Ankhinyan milaake chale nahin jana* (Having met my eyes, don't go away). How something that's romantic in one language translates into something so banal.

As we approached the outskirts of Sukkur, Nur Bux explained, "Sai, your people are quite well off. We, Mussalmans, when it comes to doing business are not good. The government here knows that, and they have given Hindu dewans free rein to run the wholesale trade. I am taking you to their mandi (market) now." He turned right, driving into a market with thirty to forty godaams (warehouses) around a huge square. In front of the shops lay heaps of grains, lentils, and dates, being filled by labourers into large brown jute sacks. The filled sacks would be transported at the end of the day by trucks to markets across Pakistan.

Nur Bux asked me to look at the people sitting outside on the chairs. He said, "These are your people, Amil and Vaniya traders. They own this." I asked him how he knew that. He said that the names in Sindhi outside the shops, written in Arabic Sindhi script on the signboards, showed their Hindu origins. They were all ages—young and old men neatly dressed in their local shalwars and long kameez shirts. As we slowly drove around the square, they looked up inquisitively at me taking their photos. I told Nur Bux to stop, and stepped out of the car to talk to them.

Approaching them, I introduced myself. They were amused at my background and invited me to sit and have tea with them. Earlier, on entering Sukkur, Nur Bux had informed me that some of the big houses we saw on the way belonged to these dewans.

Sindhi Hindus are known for their business acumen; they can be found doing commerce as far away as Africa and South America. Seeing that such a large contingent of Hindu traders had stayed on in Pakistan, I thought that there were at least some Sindhis who had paid heed to Gandhi's words on the eve of Partition: "If even a single Sindhi leaves Sindh, it will be a matter of shame to Mr Jinnah as Governor General." Then he added: "The Sindhi Hindus are first-class businessmen. Why are they running away to Bombay, Madras, and other places? It will not be they who will be the losers, but Sindh. For they will make money for themselves, wherever they go." (Malkani, p 110)

I asked these Hindu traders if they were happy in Pakistan. One of the young men from the group jovially replied: "Yes, yes, we like it here. It's where we are from. We were born here." All of them had been to India for weddings and other social occasions to meet relatives. Because of my interest in ancestral connections, I told them about my two aunts who were married to families in Old Sukkur. Again, the same reply. They were too young to know anyone born in the 1920s. They were however pleased to have a group photograph taken. The inquisitive smiles on their faces made me wonder what was running through their minds when they looked at me. Perhaps they appreciated in me, not belonging to India or Pakistan, a strong desire to claim my Sindhi connections.

We drove to the centre of the city. Nur Bux kept mentioning the names of places and streets, hoping that I might recognize something. He did not realize how little I knew about my family and their history. None of us, my cousins and I, had ever tried to seek information from our elders, since no one ever imagined that one day it might be possible for us to travel to the other side. Moreover, our interest in Sindh was not the same as that of our parents, who were born and raised there and had hoped someday to return.

Sitting with those Hindu traders reminded me of a meeting I had had some years ago at a Canadian friend's house in Toronto with a young Pakistani man who had recently emigrated with his family from Karachi. It was his mention of having been born in Karachi that drew me to him. I had never met anyone from Sindh. Irfan had an attractive demeanour. Soft-spoken, he chose his words carefully. It was when I said that Lahore was the place of my birth and my ancestors came from Sindh that he remarked that his grandparents and parents emigrated to Pakistan from India at the same time when mine might have gone to the other side. He had an ironic smile as he said, "You know, we are the two-percent people," referring to the Urdu-speakers who came to Pakistan from the northern state of UP in India. It was a difficult choice leaving behind land that might be taken over by Hindus, but there was this sense that they would be amongst Muslim brethren who, though they spoke a different language, waited for them with open arms. In the early years of settlement, the refugees had to start from scratch finding livelihood, food, and shelter. The Pakistan government had created a quota scheme in which two percent of the jobs were reserved for Urdu-speaking refugees, the Muhajirs from India.

The scheme floundered, because Muhajirs were seen as a threat by the natives. Also, religious differences among Muslims created conflicts. Due to their inability to obtain employment in government, the Muhajirs had little choice but to create for themselves alternate means of survival in the private sector. Irfan was very proud of his parents and grandparents, who had worked hard to become part of an enterprising middle class in Pakistan.

Irfan's story of the "two-percent" Urdu-speaking refugees was similar to that of my Sindhi refugee relatives on the Indian side. It was not just the similarity of being a tiny minority of entrepreneurs, but in both cases a common denominator was the ruthless uprooting from their native lands and being thrown into a geographical region which had little connection to their culture except for religion. And even there, expressions of religious devotion and rituals turned out to be different than those of their ancestral land.

Driving back on the main road into town, Nur Bux pointed to the left. "Sai, that is J B Mangharam Factory, the first large manufacturer of sweets and biscuits." This time he must have noted a glint of recognition in my eyes. Mangharam was a Sindhi industrialist whose J B Rose was one of the most popular soft drinks in North India in the 1950s, prior to the penetration of the soft-drink market by Coca Cola and Pepsi Cola. I remembered visiting the JBM factory in Gwalior, India in 1960 as part of my father's Sindhu Kala Kendra cultural troupe. We stayed at the factory guesthouse and toured the plant.

Nur Bux informed me that the Sukkur JBM plant had closed down many years ago due to some labour problem and had been lying abandoned ever since. We drove closer to the river. "This is Bundar Road (Port Road)." On the unkempt broken road was an old neglected house that once used to be the customs house. "In the old days, consignments by boat arrived here from Karachi for distribution to northern towns," Bux said.

From Bundar Road we turned left onto Station Road. We were in front of Sukkur railway station, one of the most charming little train stations I have ever seen. It had only one platform. Freshly lime-washed in white, its two adjoining arches at the entrance were painted solid blue. A few wide steps, coloured brown, led inside. Above the entrance in black, evenly spaced letters was written: SUKKUR. The façade was like a mosque, with two minarets on the sides with green calligraphy on them. It was very unusual to see such a neat and tidy

station on the subcontinent during midday, with hardly a soul around!

Further into the town, there were a couple of small parks, named after local Hindu merchants. It was interesting how Nur Bux seemed to know about all the places connected to the Hindus. The road took us down a slope to the chowk, a very busy carrefour with a high clock tower covered on the top with a pale blue onion shaped dome. It was several times taller than the one at Lakhi Dar, denoting Sukkur as a bigger town. It had an octagonal base on which were four floors with wrap-around balconies, and served both as a view tower and a minaret from which the muezzin could call the city for prayers.

I got out of the taxi to walk around the bazaar and took some photographs. There were a couple of cinema houses, with huge colourful billboards showing scenes from movies currently running in those theatres. I had a strangely familiar feeling about the square. The first movie I had ever seen was here in a cinema in Sukkur. I remember that hot summer afternoon walking with my mother and widowed aunts in the bright sun from Old Sukkur on the other side of the train station; crossing a railway underpass we went to see the matinee show at the local cinema house. After all these years the name of the film, *Ratan,* was still intact in my memory. I could see myself as a five-year-old in shorts and shirt sitting in the dark hall. The light flickering through the projection room widening into larger-than-life images of the hero and heroine Karan Dewan and Suraiya. The round-faced heroine sings *Ankhinyan milaake chale nahin jana* (Having met my eyes, don't go away).

Why images from a 1946 movie would stay so long in the mind confounded me. Perhaps it's the same with all first experiences—food, journey, music, or love. Since the 1965 war between India and Pakistan, there had been an official ban in both the countries of films from the other side. There are reports, however, that one of the first cooperative projects in the current thawing of relations between the two countries will likely be the resuming of the screening of each other's films.

Sukkur looked relatively prosperous, though it was Shikarpur that I had imagined to be full of riches. Shikarpur's reputation was as the home of the hundi-wallas of Upper Sindh, who moved money from one part of the country to the other. When I mentioned this to Nur Bux, he coyly remarked, "Sai, people of Shikarpur even today have the same reputation—very tight-fisted, who can squeeze every paisa (penny) out of your pocket without you even knowing. Some call them—'shikarpur ja shoda' (Rascals of Shikarpur)." In India, Punjabis and Sikhs were known for their valour and romance, and Sindhis for being practical businessmen and their women for being style conscious and fashion-minded. I wondered if similar stereotypes prevailed in Pakistan.

We had one more place to visit—the Hindu shrine of Sadh Belo by the river. Founded by Swami Bankhandi in 1823, it was the most prominent Sindhi Hindu shrine, situated on a small island in the river between Sukkur and Rohiri. At midday, from the riverbank, the place looked deserted. The boatman invited us to take a trip around the island, since the place was closed at noon.

The temple looked like an oasis of tranquility, a stone wall rising from the water on either side of its huge arched entrance. A number of wide stone steps led up from the water to the gate. Inside the Sadh Belo retreat, there were temples in the shades of the trees. It was already one o'clock, the sun was scorching. It was time to move on to my last destination—my father's birthplace, Rohiri.

9

Rohiri—A Town of Mystics

So much spirituality I had seen in one day that it reminded me of my father's friend Professor Motilal Butani who had lived in Rohiri. Informing me about my Upper Sindh heritage years ago, he had written, "Among the various proverbs about Rohiri, I must remind you of one—'Oh Rohiri! Even your stones must be worshipped because in the past at one time all the saints must have passed over them, graced by the touch of their feet.'" There are supposed to have been twenty-five thousand saints in Rohiri.

Nur Bux drove through Old Sukkur to get on to the steel bridge over the river. Though officially named during the British Raj as Lansdowne Bridge, the locals called it "kainchi," the Scisssors Bridge, because it could be raised in the middle to let boats with masts pass under. It was an old girder bridge without any piers. Adjacent to it was a more modern steel bridge with a semi-circular shape. It is named after Pakistan's first military ruler and appropriately called "Ayub Bridge."

As we crossed over, Nur Bux showed me a large,

ornate stepped building, six stories high. In earlier days, it was owned by Hindus. After they left, the Urdu-speaking refugees from India moved in. Rohiri had been predominantly a Hindu town before 1947.

Close to this stepped, multistoried building facing the river, the road came to an abrupt end. We were now at the foot of a hill which was densely covered with old houses built on sandstone rock. These closely nestled dwellings gave the hillock the appearance of a patched yellow and beige quilt. There was hardly a blade of grass around. Stopping the car, Nur Bux announced that we were in Rohiri.

The street approaching the treeless hill was narrow, and it was impossible to drive the taxi up into the old district. Helplessly, the driver remarked, "We must walk to the takkad."

Nur Bux wanted us to walk up towards the Chabutra crossing. I had mentioned it as a place close to where my father was born. As we marched through the old market streets, flanked on both sides by rows of small shops, Nur Bux began asking people about Vaasho vari ghitti, the street where my father and his family had once lived. It was in an area that I had heard described as "Brahminon ka Mohalla" (the neighbourhood of Brahmin priests).

Despite a grey baseball cap protecting my head from the sun, the heat of the day had begun to affect me. The streets were narrow and packed densely with rows of two-and-three-floor houses that were shabby and worn down. I felt claustrophobic in these cramped alleys. This place was considerably smaller in scale from the images of my childhood memories. I had felt the same way in Shikarpur, everything around looked much smaller than I remembered them from my visit to the area as a five-year-old.

There was a concentration of Hindu families and small shops in the old neighbourhood. As we walked by the shops, Nur Bux read the signage over the entrance of a stall, repeating the Hindu name of the owner that was neatly written in Arabic Sindhi script on the tin board. Some Hindu families in my father's quarter had decided to stay on. This might have been due to good communal relations in the area, or its proximity to Hindu shrines of Sadh Belo, which served as a sanctuary during the tumultuous times of Partition.

Like other places we had visited that morning, here too no one could remember much about the Hindus from pre-Partition days, especially those who had migrated to India. One of the younger men took us to a Hindu shopkeeper who ran an electrical repair shop. There was an air of authority about this middle-aged man. I was not sure if it came from his age or from being a community leader. He wore the traditional beige loose shirt with white stripes, and shalwar trousers.

Sitting on a wooden stool in his tiny shop, he was busy fixing an electric iron on a raised workbench. As soon as he saw us, he stood up and came down the steps of the shop. While the younger man deferentially repeated what he had heard about me from the taxi driver, the shop owner studied me with interest. After a moment's pause, he introduced himself in Sindhi, "I used to be with the Irrigation Department, an electrical engineer.

Now retired, I own this shop. Where are you from?"

I replied, "Canada, but originally a Sindhi Hindu from India." His penetrating eyes scrutinized me. I continued with my story, "My father was born here in Rohiri . . . " "Vaasho vari ghitti," he wryly repeated, confirming its existence. The word "ghitti" in Sindhi means a narrow lane. Encouraged, I said, "My grandfather's name was Ayaldas Bhaneja. He had two sons, Devidas and Sugumal. My father was the younger one, Sugumal. Both lived in the same lane along with their cousin Shri Nandlal. I visited them once when I was five years old for my oldest cousin's wedding." Nur Bux intervened, bringing the conversation to the present. "Sai," he addressed the shopkeeper, "this sahib has enough time. He has to catch his train from Rohiri Station at 10:30 tonight."

Then he added, "It is getting quite hot. I suggest you pass the rest of the day here; you can walk around to find your family house and then spend the rest of the time in the temple by the river. You will find it interesting."

The shopkeeper gave a sharp look at the driver, mumbling under his breath that the driver was pulling a fast one on me. He asked me, "Where are you going next?" I replied, "Lahore. I was born there." The man then told the driver, "Okay, you leave him here. We will take care of Sai and show him everything." While all this was going on, I noticed a small crowd gathered around, curiously examining me, wondering how all this would end. Nur Bux glanced in my direction to check if I was satisfied with what was being proposed.

I felt like a bundle being exchanged, in the middle of

nowhere. I was apprehensive. How was I to discern who was friend or foe, a Hindu or a Muslim? My unease was about not wanting to end up with the wrong people.

Years earlier when my wife and I visited India, we were travelling by bus from Ajanta caves to Aurangabad when we saw a group of men befriending a young Japanese tourist who was travelling with us. The next morning we found the youth in the hotel lobby in tears having lost all his belongings. His new friends had slipped him a sleeping potion in a drink. I remember him saying that he never thought that there would be such deceit and thievery in the land of Mahatma Gandhi. That had taught me the important lesson of being careful who you fraternized with when travelling.

The shopkeeper seemed to understand my hesitation. "Don't worry, Sai," he said in a firm voice. "We will drop you at the station to catch the Karakoram Express for Lahore. It is always late. You are our guest."

He let me know what plan he had in mind: "We will first go to our local Vasan Shah shrine, a wedding lunch is being hosted by the bride's family. From there, I will take you to my house. You will meet my family and we will have something to eat together. Then you take some rest. In the evening we will go for a stroll, and later we will drop you at the station."

I knew I had a quick decision to make. Should I spend a few more hours with Nur Bux, who would have driven me around Rohiri and later left me on my own at the train station for the rest of the day? I would end up in the railway waiting room until the train arrived. The other choice was the one offered by this total stranger I had just met. But then as far as I was concerned everyone was a stranger in Sindh. Ultimately, it is our faith in ourselves that makes us decide at such moments whether to take the risk.

Despite my fears, I gave in to the shopkeeper's invitation.

Smiling, Nur Bux assured me, "Nothing to worry, Sai. You are with your own people."

The shopkeeper called a boy in the crowd and told him to go with Nur Bux to the river to bring my duffle bag from the taxi. I paid Nur Bux the fare and thanked him for the splendid work he had done in showing me the three towns. The boy disappeared with Nur Bux down the lane to fetch the duffle bag. The small crowd that had gathered around us slowly dispersed in different directions.

The shopkeeper asked me my name. I told him, and in return asked his. "Bhajan Lal Bhatia," he replied. There was pride in the way he spoke his name. "Everyone in Rohiri knows me. Ask anyone my name and they will recognize it. I have been sent letters by post from all over the world with just my name and "Rohiri" on them, and would you believe it, they reach me." I was familiar with the Bhatia surname. While growing up in our refugee colony in Delhi, there were two Brahmin Bhatia brothers from Rohiri who were my father's acquaintances. They had arrived from Pakistan at Partition and moved into our neighbourhood. The older of the two brothers had been my father's teacher in Rohiri. My host said that it so happened that his two sisters were also teachers, and they might have heard about the Bhatia brothers.

"Do you like movies?" Surprised, I nodded. He continued: "I have the largest movie collection in Sindh: 790 classics in videos and DVDs. This is my greatest hobby. You can see any movie you want at my place." I was impressed.

Someone dropped by to buy an electric plug, another one stood in front on the street wanting to pick up the iron he had left for repair. While putting the repaired iron in a plastic bag, Bhajan Lal told the man to stop by at his house on the way and to tell his wife that he was bringing home a visitor from India for lunch. In the meantime, the boy had returned carrying my duffle bag. Bhajan Lal asked him to put the bag at the back of the shop. Then he announced to me, "In your honour, Sai, I am going to close the shop for the rest of the day. It will give us some time together." He added, "The shop is just a way to kill time. One iron a day to repair, that's enough to keep me going. I get enough from my pension." His authority came from his firm voice, which became friendlier the more he spoke to me. His dyed auburn hair, like that of older men in the region, made his face look younger. He suggested that I leave the bag at the shop until the evening; this would make it easier for us to walk around the town. I decided however to carry along my knapsack containing my train tickets and water bottle.

Bhajan Lal pulled the steel shutter down and locked the shop with a big padlock. We walked back on the lane towards the river on our way to Sai Vasan Shah's temple. He had to make a social appearance there, the family of the bride having invited him to the communal lunch in the temple compound. As we entered the compound, I could see that it was a much larger building than I had anticipated. There were about fifty guests present.

Despite the event being hosted by the bride's family, there were no women present. I could not imagine a Sindhi bridal luncheon in India without women. Perhaps things had not changed much here since olden times. The lunchtime festivity was friendly and jovial; a photographer was taping the event for the marriage video and DVD. People seemed to know Bhajan Lal well. He continuously introduced me to people, but the introductions were too quick and short to enable any meaningful exchanges about the past or present.

Bhajan Lal then rushed me into the temple so I could pay my respects at Vasan Shah's shrine. I was familiar with Sai Vasan Shah's photograph; the same picture was on the altar of my uncle Devidas's home in Delhi. In the photograph the holy man sits barechested in a white loincloth on a wooden bench. He has shoulder-length hair, and the eyes from his gaunt face pierce the viewer. Sai Vasan Shah, like most fakir saints, was known to have performed miracles. Upper Sindh was full of stories of such phenomena.

Some of these mystics in tattered garments with unshaven faces were said to have been clairvoyant. Vasan Shah and Baba Nebhraj were among those in Sindh who stayed, having foretold tragic happenings, such as Mahatma Gandhi's assassination and the partition of the subcontinent. Baba Nebhraj is known to have referred to Mahatma Gandhi as that "langoti walla" (the loin-cloth wearer), identifying him as a true fakir brother. For them to leave their homeland and move to India as refugees was out of the question. Their followers until the last moment could not persuade them to leave.

Bhajan Lal took me upstairs to show me the newly constructed guest house on top of the temple. From here one had a panoramic view of the river to the south, including the Lansdowne Bridge, the island of Sadh Belo, and in the distance the huge Sukkur Barrage spanning the Indus. In the north the ink-blue water stretched to the bend by a dry hillock. "Next time you come, you can stay here for free." Bhajan Lal gave a hearty laugh.

Standing on the terrace I thought about my father and his love for water and rivers and especially his Republic Day project of Jhuley Lal—seeds for such aspirations were sown at this point. The marriage party below reminded me of my newlywed parents arriving in Rohiri, visiting this family shrine first. They must have used this place for pooja blessings when they left Rohiri for Lahore, Karachi, and Bombay in those pre-Partition days.

Next, Bhajan Lal and I retraced our steps uphill, passing by small side streets. The only traffic was a tonga buggy, a three-wheeler auto. As we turned left into a narrow lane, which could barely accommodate three persons walking together, a stinking open drain flowing on both sides, Bhajan Lal asked me if I recognized it. We were at the mouth of Vaasho vari ghitti. It was the lane in which my father's family had once lived.

In my mind it was a much wider and longer street. In my hazy picture of the past, the lane branched from the street, sloping leftwards and ending at the river. Somewhere in the middle were three modest brick row houses of the Bhaneja clan. There was a well in front of the house and a bit further, near the river, a grottolike small Shiva temple. In the pantheon of Indian gods and goddesses, along with Jhuley Lal it was Shiva and Durga Devi who were the most common family deities that one heard about among the Hindu families of Sindh. I remembered how my grandmother would go out at dusk to float the little jyoti lamps of flour dough on the river—I could see rows of these lit-up floats drifting with the water's flow southward, as women prayed to the God of the Indus River, Jhuley Lal. Strangely, I was also reminded of a lingering smell from those days, of mustard and coconut oils used for either moistening a dry scalp or for massaging the torso before bathing by the well or in the river.

I had learnt, through the "family tree" my uncle had put together, that my ancestry went back to the eighteenth century, when our clan was believed to have lived here in the so-called neighbourhood of Brahmins. In actuality, they belonged to the Khatri caste, whose members had worked as court bailiffs, locomotive drivers, building contractors, cloth merchants, jewellers, and goldsmiths. Later on, I came to learn that Hindu Sindhis, unlike the rest of India, were a casteless community with two dominant groups, the Bhaibund, whose ancestors were essentially businessmen and traders, and the Amil, who were civil servants in royal courts and civil administrations. In modern times they had taken on a wide variety of professions.

Bhajan Lal explained that over the years the new owners and their families had divided and joined properties in different configurations in the neighbourhood. Some had demolished the old row houses and others had built additions on top of the old ones. He recalled that there used to be a well, but its mouth was closed when it ran out of water. Yes, there was a Shivala, a temple to God Shiva. Since there was no pujari or priest to look after it, it soon fell into disuse. He did not remember Hindu women ever going for worship to the river after Partition. This had become overnight a neighbourhood in which Muhajir migrants from India had moved in. The newcomers brought their own customs and ways.

I asked him, "Are you not afraid to live here as a tiny minority?"

"Not at all," he boldly replied. "We were born here. This is our neighbourhood."

I had heard a similar reply earlier in Sukkur from the young Hindu trader. There was a sense of pride and belongingness to the soil in that remark. Before 1947, Hindus comprised over 25 percent of Sindh's population; after Partition the Hindu minority of the province dwindled to between 1 to 2 percent—still the largest number of Hindus of Pakistan lived in Sindh. As Nur Bux had said, Sindhi Hindus were known for their trade and business acumen. There had been, however, reports in the media about extortions and kidnappings of Hindu traders and even murders of those involved in political work in the Larkana-Sukkur corridor. Two hundred

Hindu families lived in Rohiri, and around the same number in Shikarpur.

Bhajan Lal said, "You are asking interesting questions. Let's go home. My older sister may be able to help with your queries about your father's teacher friends. She used to be a school teacher."

We crossed the street into another narrow lane. The town was a maze of small gulleys and lanes. Bhajan Lal pressed the buzzer at the door of his house. A narrow stone staircase led to a flat above. The house faced an old but well-maintained Shia mosque. At its narrow entrance, on the top of the green gate, was written in large black letters in English, Dargah Gate Mosque.

Bhajan Lal informed me that I had arrived in Rohiri on an important Muslim day, in the month of Moharram. On this day, Shias mourned and commemorated the martyrdom of their founder Hussain Ibn Ali, killed in the battle of Karbala. As I had never experienced Moharram before, Bhajan Lal thought I would find the ceremony of mourning to be of interest.

On entering the Bhatia family's living room, I joined my palms together to extend my Indian namaste greetings. The room was painted light blue and filled with chairs, sofa, shelves, cupboards, and a cot. On the wall hung a calendar advertising a gas stove from a local company. Mr Bhatia's wife, daughter, and oldest sister were all there. It was three o'clock. When his wife complained about why it had taken him so long to come home for lunch, Bhajan Lal went into the details of all the places he had shown me so far. Covering her head with a dupatta, Mrs Bhatia apologized for her husband, saying that he had a tendency to forget the time when he chatted with people. She had a cheerful round face. While she hurried into the kitchen to prepare a hot meal, Bhajan Lal introduced me to his older sister. The middle-aged lady wearing a floral print dress examined me with some curiosity. He asked her if she knew about the two Bhatia brothers from pre-Partition days. No luck. I inquired about her life as a teacher.

The literacy rate in Sindh was supposed to be the highest in Pakistan. Bhajan Lal's sister had recently retired as the principal of the local girls' school. This seemed incredible, for my image of Hindus in Pakistan, at least Hindu Sindhis, belied this. To reach the position of a principal, she must have spent years in the government educational system in various teaching positions. Later I would meet Bhajan Lal's other sister, who worked as a divisional officer in the local Board of Education. This was impressive, as the official literacy rate in Pakistan was stated to be around 46 percent, of which the male literacy rate was higher (60 percent) compared to the female (32 percent) rate. Sindhi Hindu women from a middle-class family employed in pensioned government positions seemed an admirable feat and it spoke well of pluralism in the country.

A meal was being laid out for the two of us on a low wooden table covered with a cloth and plastic table mats. The meal comprised of saayi bhaji (spinach), dhal (lentils), chappatis, and rice with kachri and papads all cooked in traditional Sindhi style. There was something surreal about sitting in that old city home just a stone's throw from where my father was born, eating a Sindhi meal in the home of a Hindu family. That morning at the motel I had wondered if I would be able to find a morsel to eat during the day, now here I was at this family table breaking bread with Bhajan Lal and his family.

Mrs Bhatia asked me in Sindhi, "How has the day been so far?"

I told her about where I had been since morning and the reason for visiting all those places. She was a friendly woman with a sparkle in her eye. Pleased to hear about my mother's connection with Shikarpur, she said, "My family is also from Shikarpur. I was born there."

Delighted, I asked,"The family name?"

She replied: "Katarias." I was hoping she might have some connection with the Lalwanis, the family name on my maternal side.

When we finished lunch, Bhajan Lal looked at me. "Please take some rest. You must be tired. I will show you to your room. It is nice and cool there. You will be able to rest. I will take you around for a walk of the neighbourhood in the evening. You have plenty of time for your train." Almost six hours, I noticed, as I glanced at my watch.

We walked over to the room next door. It was large with a high ceiling but surprisingly no windows. My host turned on the electric fan and showed me the bed. For a moment, in a room without a window, I felt claustrophobic, but soon I got used to it. I had been told elsewhere that the absence of windows in houses in olden times was to prevent men from looking at young women inside (or vice versa, I assumed). I was marvelling at this totally unexpected attention I was receiving in my ancestral neighbourhood. Lying on that bed in the room by myself, I imagined my father as a young boy returning from school on a hot afternoon. His Ammi would serve him the kind of meal I had just finished. After his meal, to avoid the heat of the day, as I was doing now, he would have been told by his mother to lie down for a siesta.

I wondered why one family like my father's chose to leave their homeland, while another like Bhajan Lal's stayed despite the overnight demographic shift in their little town. I thought about the Bhatias—how the family had stuck together in the land of their birth inspite of the upheaval and finding themselves among a tiny minority in their native place. Bhajan Lal seemed happy with the choice his parents had made. The few Hindus whom I had met during the day mentioned that it was difficult for their parents to abandon their small businesses and properties—to leave everything behind and move to India. Perhaps the Bhatias thought that once the communal unrest had subsided everything would be normal again, and all those who left for India would come back.

What makes us stay or leave our homelands forever? There is a belief in the Hindu scriptures that without the will of God, not a leaf on a tree moves. Often the reason is beyond our control, a political-historical event, but sometimes the decision to leave comes from a desire to make a life elsewhere, or simply to see the world. I remember once asking my Canadian friends how their families ended up in Canada from different parts of the world. Interestingly, the reply in most cases was that the move was related to one particular individual who had already come to Canada. In the case of my father's family, it was his home in Delhi that made everyone from his clan head there in 1947. Perhaps the Bhatia family and many others like them did not have anyone to go to in India.

My father left Rohiri fifteen years before Partition, working in Dadu, Karachi, Lahore, Bombay, and finally Delhi. He could never see himself as just a Sindhi tied to Rohiri, though he loved Sindh and his hometown. He saw himself as an Indian beyond an exclusively regional identity. For his after-dinner evening walks, putting away his work outfit of starched shirt and trousers, he would get into a casual dhoti, shalwar, or a pyjama-kurta and carry himself in the way of a Punjabi, a Bengali, or a Hindi-speaker. As a man involved with culture and theatre, dressing the "Indian way" came naturally to him.

Questions kept popping in my head. I wondered why I had felt the compulsion to come all the way from Canada to Upper Sindh. This was not a casual holiday. Something within me had been coaxing me for years to visit Sindh one day. Perhaps it was a sense of dharma, or duty. As the eldest son, I had with my two younger brothers Suresh and Harish performed the final rites for both my parents by the holy Ganges. With Suresh, I had travelled from Delhi to Haridwar ("Gateway to God") for their "pinda" ceremony, followed by the ash immersion into the holy river. But these final rites and the dip in the holy waters had not brought inner tranquility—a sense of filial duty had continued to gnaw at me two decades after their passing. I had to come this far to my parent's native land to fulfil their longing to be home at least once. Bhajan Lal's family was in a way right to have stayed back. Is it not true that ultimately, our emotions, our feelings, our spirit are connected to the place to which we belong, where we were born? Happiest is the man who does not have to leave his homeland. Tired, thinking all this, I fell asleep in the cool breeze from the fan.

A knock at the door awakened me. It was Bhajan Lal's daughter.

"Uncle, Papa asked me if you would like to have tea?"

"Thank you, I would love that." I was quite comfortable with Bhajan Lal's daughter calling me "Uncle," as it is customary to address elders this way whether they are related to us or not.

Bhajan Lal's daughter was in her late teens. I was curious. "Are you studying?"

"Yes, Uncle," she replied. "I am doing BSc in chemistry."

"That's impressive. You must be bright."

Becoming self-conscious at my compliment, the girl vigorously shook her head. "I plan to change from chemistry to law next year. I want to be a lawyer." Then she quickly disappeared to bring the tea.

Shortly afterwards Bhajan Lal came in to ask me if I would like to freshen up. He showed me the washroom. When I returned, he had taken out his video collection. His daughter left tea and biscuits on the table. I was hoping that we would not get into watching the films, as I wanted to go out to walk in the town. But when he offered to show me a Sindhi feature film on Bhagat Kanwar Ram made by the Pakistani KTN network, it was difficult to say no. I had never seen a Sindhi movie, not to mention one about this particular Sindhi icon. It seemed that the trip I had taken in order to capture my roots was meant to become a total immersion into my spiritual heritage.

Like Sai Vasan Shah, Bhagat Kanwar Ram (1883–1939) was a saint from Upper Sindh. Wearing a long white gown and red turban, he was known as a singer-saint who danced while singing in the tradition of the Sufis. He was among the first Sindhi singers recorded by HMV between 1920 and 1930. In total, he had twenty-one Sindhi devotional songs recorded on HMV 78 rpm records.

Bhajan Lal put on the Kanwar Ram DVD for me. The film, directed and acted by Muslim artists, was shot in colour on locations across Sindh, where the saint-singer had lived. It showed how this man of gentle nature was drawn to God and discovered his divinity through works of love and service. He would go from village to village singing devotional songs in his high-pitched voice in the night raga of Sindh called Bhairavi. The film showed Kanwar Ram as a married man, leading a normal life as a craftsman, not using public contributions for personal needs. His melodious singing in the open squares every evening after supper drew large crowds eager to listen to him.

On one such occasion, a woman placed her child in his arms and asked him to sing a lullaby to it. She did not tell him that the baby, wrapped in clothing, was dead. His lullaby is said to have brought the baby back to life. The movie showed this episode from the saint's life accompanied by the famous song, *O Naale alakh je bero taar muhinjo* (O Lord, keep this boat of my life afloat). Bhagat Kanwar Ram was born in Jarvaran, Sindh, in April 1883 and died from the gun shots of a fanatic Muslim at Ruk railway station on 2 November 1939. Hindus and Muslims gathered in Sukkur to express their sorrow and anger; everything was closed down across Sindh for one week.

By the time the video was over, it had become dark outside. The street lights had come on. It looked as if we would not be able to go for our stroll. Bhajan Lal assured me that watching the Maatam mourning procession from his balcony would be more interesting.

He was keen to know my reaction to the film. It was a very true to account of the saint's life, a realistic portrayal of customs and rituals, an interesting glimpse into the Sindh of pre-Partition days. Though it was coproduced by a local merchant called Jai Ram Das, Bhajan Lal noted with admiration that the Hindu characters in the film were played by Muslim actors. The film did not hesitate to show the violence by Muslim communalists that the minority Hindus had to bear. "These things," he said, "happen once in a while here as well as in India. One has to find ways to prevent them." Since its release the movie has been widely shown on local and national television channels across Pakistan. This was one of the first initiatives aimed at promoting intercommunal harmony in recent years. Bhajan Lal insisted that I take the DVD with me as a Rohiri souvenir. The cover showed pictures of the film director Hussain Shaikh and writers Ayub Gul and Loung Shaikh.

A second round of tea was brought in by Bhajan Lal's daughter.

I said, "Mr Bhatia, this girl tells me that she is going to be a lawyer, not a chemist."

Bhajan Lal laughed. "Yes, she wants to be like her father, argumentative."

"Yes, after my BSc, I will do my LLB." She made her point.

As she left the room, Bhajan Lal casually said, "She can do law if she likes, I have no problem with that." He took a deep sigh and then looked at me as if he wanted to confide in me about something. "You know, I had an older daughter. She died two years ago. Like her, she was a very bright student. She would have been a medical doctor today. They (the hospital doctors) botched up the surgery."

His face had saddened, his voice quivered.

It was disconcerting to see someone who had looked so confident a moment ago, now struggling to hold back tears. I could feel his hurt. I took his hand and pressed it gently. I remembered that someone had given me a small sachet of sacred ash for good luck while I was visiting the Sathya Sai Baba Ashram in South India. I took it out from my knapsack and placed it in his hand. "Keep it, please. It will give you solace."

While I was searching for the sachet, I had felt my father's book and the audio cassette of the two Motihar brothers in the knapsack. This was the place, I decided, where the two mementos should be left. I handed them to Bhajan Lal as keepsakes. He looked a bit puzzled. He took the book and quickly browsed through it. I mentioned my father, "He was born here." Bhajan Lal read the listing of songs and poets on the cover. Somehow he seemed to have understood their sentimental meaning. He put the two mementos aside. I could feel the presence of my parents' spirit in that house, in that neighbourhood, and in those narrow crooked lanes of old Rohiri.

There were many questions I wanted to raise about the politics of living as a minority but I resisted. This was not a journalist's trip, rather it was a journey about paying homage to my roots, my ancestors, and my parents. The day spent with the family had, in many ways, answered most of the questions in my mind.

It had gotten dark. Walking through the streets of Rohiri at that late evening hour was not possible. Under the starry night sky, Bhajan Lal and I stood on the balcony of his home to watch the dimly lit narrow street. There was a gentle warm breeze swirling through the lane. A crowd of men dressed in black had begun to assemble outside the mosque for the Shia Muslim mourning called Maatam. Bhajan Lal said that the men were gathered to form a remembrance procession, grieve the martyred deaths of Imam Hussein and his family thirteen hundred years ago in a battle in Karbala, Iraq. There was a white stallion standing without a rider, representing the leader's horse and a Tazia made of colourful strips of paper in the shape of a pyramid, his mausoleum. Before the procession began, a young man in the midst of the crowd holding a microphone began to sing a lament, reciting the Shia martyrs' story. There were no musical instruments accompanying the tenor's sonorous voice. The strikingly gentle horse, unlike the decorated ones used in local weddings to carry the bridegroom, had no ornamental bridle adorning it. In absence of decorations, the stallion's diamond shaped sad eyes made the animal's long face look even more sorrowful.

As the procession began to move, led by the white horse, a hundred or so mourners followed, beating their chests—some with batons—and chanting in unison, "Hai Hassan, Hai Hussein." The last section of the procession carried the floral Tazia on their shoulders. The sound of the wailing echoed in the gully. We watched the procession march ahead till it disappeared at the end of the lane in the darkness of the night.

I was reminded of an incident from my childhood, in which the Muslim family of my little friends Suraiya and Kasim in our Lodhi Colony quarters had disappeared overnight into hiding to protect themselves in the Karbala ruins of Aliganj. I never saw them again. I wonder if they ever made it to Pakistan with their parents. Is God another name for fate, which has at every corner a surprising event waiting for us, a happy or a sad one? "Do you believe in God?" was a pointed question put to me years ago in London in one of my diplomatic postings by the elderly editor of the UK Parliamentary journal, *Science and Parliament,* Maurice Goldsmith. Do you believe in God? How does one answer such a personal question posed by someone you barely know, during a working lunch? I was surprised at my reply: "I assume if I did not believe in God, then I would have to be egotistical." Maurice had nodded wisely, and we had continued with our meal. Two years later this new friend succumbed to cancer. I wondered if he knew of his cancer when we met over lunch . . .

It was about time to leave for the railway station. My cousin Uttam and his wife Rani, with whom I was staying in Delhi, had asked me if I could bring the specialty fruit adh kharak from Sindh. They had for years craved these half-cut dried dates, not having tasted them since childhood. When I mentioned this to Mrs Bhatia, she said there were some in the house. She quickly ran into the kitchen to bring them and stuffed them into a large envelope which she gave to me, saying, "Your relatives in Delhi will be very pleased."

I was moved by the generosity of the Bhatia household. I remembered Abida Parveen's brother telling me in Islamabad, "Sai, they will take you in your lap and not let you go."

Insisting that I would depart by myself I took the three-wheeler autorickshaw flagged down for me on the lane to the train station. It seemed to me as if through some special grace Bhajan Lal had lifted me from the street and treated me with such kindness; now he had let me go. My final memory of the Bhatias is the whole family standing in the courtyard upstairs: Bhajan Lal, his wife, his son, daughter, and daughter-in-law with the grandchild in her arms, wishing me goodbye.

10

Rohiri Junction

There is an endearing image of my mother at this station seared in my mind; an inexperienced teenage bride, she is carrying her first-born, Buley, in her arms on the way to her husband's new home in Karachi.

In the darkness the autorickshaw weaved through the faintly lit streets of the old town. We passed by long rows of shops in the bazaar that were closed down for the day. In front of the shops, people were rolling out their beddings to prepare for sleeping outdoors. I was euphoric. Despite my fears I had made the right decision to accept Bhajan Lal's invitation to spend the afternoon with his family.

The long afternoon with the Bhatia family felt like a dream. A visit to Rohiri was something that my parents had always longed for, and the knowledge that I had done so would have pleased them immensely. They would have been happy to see me in their old neighbourhood, in the land of their birth, the land of our ancestors. You never know the importance of a chance meeting, or the direction it will take you.

At the foot bridge of the railway station, the autorickshaw stopped with a jerk. As I stepped out from the vehicle, porters in red uniforms swarmed around to carry my duffle bag. Though I did not need help, I caved in as the Karakoram Express came in at the farthest platform and handed the bag over.

There were only a few passengers at that time of night on the platforms. Tea stalls with bright fluorescent lights glimmered in the darkness. Steam puffed out from the large aluminum tea kettles on the counters. The Karakoram Express was to arrive at Platform 1. I looked at the ticket booked in Rawalpindi, where under my name my wagon number and sleeper berth were indicated. The porter pointed to the location where the coach would stop, towards the northern end of the platform, and I let him go.

Sitting on the iron bench by the railway foot bridge, I could see across the tracks passengers waiting for the train to Karachi. This station had been my parents' take-off point into the outside world, which in their days was first Karachi, then Lahore, where I was born. From there, they moved to Bombay in 1942. I was on this platform with my parents only once, in 1946, on our way to Lahore and Bombay. We had changed into an express train in Lahore, called something like "Frontier Mail." It went down to Bombay via Delhi.

There was a young woman in Sindhi dress and a white headscarf sitting on the bench on the opposite platform holding a baby in her arms, who reminded me of my young mother. The oldest photograph in our family album of Mummy and Daddy is dated July 1944. In that photograph, in sepia tone, Daddy is in a light cotton suit wearing a tie on a buttoned-up shirt, Mummy is in a plain white sari. Both are wearing the round horn-rimmed glasses of the time. There is directness in my mother's gaze that comes from simplicity and a child-like straightforward manner.

Daddy was twenty-nine then and Mummy, I suppose, in her early twenties. In fact she did not know the date of her birth. She was the only one in the family who never received a birthday card. After coming to Canada, I tried to compensate for this by sending her a Mother's Day card every May. In the pre-Partition days, no one kept records of girls' birthdays except in the horoscopes retained in some families. Even when these were available, after the girl's betrothal the horoscopes were not deemed to be of much use in her new family. On top of that, it was an onerous task to reconcile the dates of birth in Hindu charts written in Sanskrit with the dates in Christian calendars. Women from my mother's era were mostly homemakers, dressed modestly, their heads covered in public with a scarf. I never saw my mother using make-up or perfume. The only cosmetic, if I could call it such, was a popular brand of talcum powder in a slim tin container. Once I had explained to her the custom of sending a card on Mother's Day to express honour and respect for mothers, Mummy started looking forward to the cards from me and my siblings every May.

In that image of my mother at this station, her father has come to put her on the train in a ladies compartment for the overnight journey. Only on her arrival at

Karachi station the next morning does she discover that the infant she has been carrying in her arms had died. Buley had stopped breathing sometime during the journey. He was born a couple of years before me. In all, my mother had nine children. Four lived, five died. Of those who survived, three were boys, one a girl.

The last time I saw my mother was in our Lajpat Nagar home in New Delhi. It was three years after my father's death. As she was suffering from osteoporosis, she was confined to bed and had to be carried from one place to another. I had come home from Canada to spend some time with her. I recall one summer night as we lay on our charpoys in the courtyard and I could hear her labouring to inhale. I reminisced.

"Mummy, those musical gatherings Daddy and you used to have on full-moon nights. I wonder if we will ever see them again."

"No one has time now. Everyone says they are busy, as if no one was busy before." Over the years, she had acquired a matriarchal tone that came with having three daughters-in-law and five grandchildren.

"Ah! It's so nice out here in the open," I heard her saying. "I am glad you came. You should have brought Marie and the boys."

"Next time," I said.

I could hear her mutter, as if saying, We will see.

To cheer her up, I mentioned the colour photograph that my sister Damayanti had taken of her the last time she was home.

"Which one?" she asked, testing me to make sure that I was not lying.

"The one in which you are wearing a white pyjama dress and holding flowers."

"I liked that one too." She was pleased. "Daman was making such a fuss about those flowers. She wanted me to hold them properly to get all the matching colours in the picture."

"You look very nice in that photo."

She looked at me intently in the dark, then changing the subject, she said, "Every time I see you, you look more and more like your father. Your sister was saying the same. You loved him a lot."

"Yes, I did." I nodded, thinking that those whom you love always remain with you in spirit.

"Do you love your mother too?"

I did not know how to respond.

She quickly rephrased herself, asking me in her rasping voice, "I meant when I die, will you still remember me?"

Was it a complaint or an appeal? I lay there in stunned silence. I wanted to hold her frail body in my arms and say, I love you, Mother, but felt awkward. It would have seemed contrived. Uneasily, I replied: "Mummy, how can one ever forget one's mother."

My mother died that summer. I wished I could have been by her side, the same way I had wished I could have been by my father at his end. My father passed away in an intensive care unit in Ottawa while I was posted in Bonn, my mother died in New Delhi at home when I was in New York on official business.

My reverie was broken by the sound of an approaching train as the Karakoram Express rolled into the station. I got up to board it and searched for my sleeper seat in the first-class wagon. In the pale blue light inside the compartment, it was one of the lower berths in the six-berth cabin. Everyone inside was asleep. As the train left Rohiri, I slid into the empty lower berth. In my duffle bag I had the Sindhi chaddar Ali had presented me in Islamabad. Using the duffle bag as a pillow, I pulled the chaddar over me.

The day had unfolded in a mysterious way. There was a lot to process from the past twenty-four hours. Images of the river, the holy shrines, Nur Bux, the narrow streets, the Bhatia family, and the white stallion from the Moharram procession in the dimly lit lane flashed through my mind. Memories of holding onto my parents' hand as a five-year-old coming down the stairs from Rohiri station's railway bridge to the platform; Mummy carrying dead Buley in her arms in the ladies compartment on the train to Karachi . . . the recollections persisted, making my heart leaden, pining for all those departed.

In real life, a perfect farewell, holding dying parents in our arms is rare; it takes place mostly in novels and movies. Parting happens arbitrarily in its own time, without one's ability to control the shape or direction of those final moments. I felt a growing ache in the pit of my stomach. A surge of loneliness engulfed me. For the first time I sensed the sorrow my mother must have felt, seeing all of her children leave India one by one forever, and finally even losing her husband in a distant foreign land. I wanted badly to hold my dead parents in my arms. Turning my face to the side, I felt a deep sob choke my throat and tears rolled down my cheeks.

11

The Train to Lahore

There had been too many stories of kidnappings and murder in Pakistan, most recently of Daniel Pearl, the *Wall Street Journal* correspondent who was killed by his young kidnappers in Karachi. I had been warned by friends and family to keep personal safety ahead of everything in my travels to Pakistan. It was common knowledge that all Islamic "terrorists," Taliban and Laskhar-e-Taiba, had their training in madrasa schools described as "terrorist factories." Can dogma also be faith? How did one distinguish the followers of dogma from the followers of a faith?

I looked at my watch, it was six o'clock in the morning. The jolt with which the train had lurched had awakened me. We were leaving a station. The sign at the platform read Khanewal. The misty light of dawn penetrated through the train window. The young fellow sleeping on the berth facing me greeted me warmly: "Salaam-a-lekum!" I reciprocated, "Wa-lekum salaam." He had a fair complexion and a handsome round face. A thin crescent-shaped beard ran from one ear to the other. He put on his white prayer cap. Standing up, he called out to his friends on the upper berths to wake up, it was time for the morning namaz. From the language and accent, I could figure out that these youths were neither Punjabi nor Sindhi, they probably were the children of Urdu-speaking Muslims who had emigrated from northern India.

Soon all five of them were standing in the space between the berths in the cabin. Obviously it was too narrow a space for everyone to pray together, so a couple of them decided to move outside into the corridor. They spread out their neatly folded prayer mats on the floor to offer their first namaz of the day. In rows of two, their mats side by side, standing up, sitting down, rising with folded hands they repeated, "Allaho Akbar!"

The five youth had the same ear-to-ear beards and wore similar perforated skullcaps. I peeked outside in the corridor to check if this was a normal routine for all Muslims. I couldn't see anyone else across the whole coach entreating God so early in the morning. After namaz, they returned to the cabin, taking their seats, two on my side and three across.

One of the young men suddenly stood up to close the door of our cabin. Saying "Bismillah–ir–rahman-ir raheem," he launched into what he called "baat," a homily on "yakin"—the Absolute Belief. This was a completely new experience for me. Nonstop the youth went on for the next fifteen to twenty minutes explaining the significance of faith and the importance of infallible belief in one's life. He gave examples from the Holy Koran of incidents of piety and sacrifice. There was not much more I could comprehend, as I had no familiarity with the Muslim scripture. I heard the leader saying that his homily was strictly for contemplation, not discussion. A fish out of water, I began to feel uneasy, wanting to escape that confined space. I wondered how the group would react if they knew that I was a Hindu of Indian origin and a former Canadian diplomat.

After their baat, one of them politely asked me, "You boarded the train last night at Rohiri?"

Keeping my composure, I replied: "Yes."

"Are you going to Lahore?"

I turned the question around, "And you all?"

"Pindi." He grinned. Rawalpindi.

"You are from Karachi?" I asked innocently.

"And you, Sir?"

"Both Rohiri and Lahore, you might say."

The youth sensed my discomfort. The same caution had overcome me when I first met Nur Bux and Bhajan Lal. A strange instinct urged me to remain silent. I was afraid that I might be asked to join in their religious chat. I turned my face away to look outside the window at the changing scenery. Was I afraid, or just being cautious? The train chugged on. None of the youths returned to their berths. Since it was day now, obviously everyone would sit on the lower berths. I was feeling squeezed, sitting between my fellow passengers.

Noticing an empty seat outside in the corridor, I stood up to offer my seat, suggesting that this would give them more room. They seemed happy and I carried my duffle bag with me into the passage. I heard the glass door quickly shut behind me.

Sitting outside in the corridor seat, I was not happy with my decision to move out of the cabin. Why did I not just stay and converse with them? How could I let pass an opportunity to engage those youths in a conversation? I generally enjoyed talking to strangers, curious to learn about other cultures. On top of that, their Urdu accent was that of Delhiwallas and one that I had always loved; it was the Urdu of the poet Mirza Ghalib, reminding me of my college days in Delhi. In my vocation as a diplomat, building relationships came naturally to me; and in my postdiplomatic career, which now focussed on promoting a culture of peace, transcending national boundaries and viewing everyone as the children of the same God had been an important goal. Their orthodox dress and behaviour, however, had made me suspect that they might belong to some religious madrasa. In my writings I had said that fear based on distrust usually comes from stereotypes. And here I was falling victim to one.

The question that bothered me for a long time was, just who then were "my people"?—Hindus, Muslims, Sindhis, Punjabis, Indians, Pakistanis, Canadians? Had I stayed home in Delhi and married a girl from the same caste and Sindhi origins, things would still not likely be any different. I would still have been unsure of the strangers with whom I was travelling. The question about my identity and that of my people has always been ambiguous. Partition had mercilessly fractured that notion of certainty about my anchor in a place and time, making me forever more cautious and quieter.

These young Muslim men could simply have been

devout believers—I don't think I would have hesitated the same way had I had a similar encounter with Hindu or Christian youths. I wondered if this inability to reach out said more about me or reflected the general human condition in the year 2006.

The Karakoram Express chugged along towards Lahore. Morning sunshine penetrated through the fog, its brilliant rays gradually burning the mist away, revealing ripe bushels of wheat in the fields. The train was passing by a small station called Kot Radha Kishan. I had read in one of the guidebooks on Lahore that there was a square named there after the Hindu goddess of wealth, Lakshmi. It was called Lakshmi Chowk. In India, however, the general view was that in Pakistan all places with Hindu names had been changed to Muslim ones. Kot Radha Kishan, another stereotype broken. My destination was still an hour from Kot Radha Kishan.

At Lahore Junction as I stepped down from the train, I saw the youth who had slept across from me in my cabin waving at me from the train window. Cheerfully he shouted, "Allah Hafiz!" I was a bit taken aback by his warm goodbye. Without any eye contact, I feebly lifted my left hand, mumbling "Khuda Hafiz" in response. Hurriedly blending into the crowd, I walked towards the exit gate to the city. I wished I had had the nerve to talk to those Muslim youths.

12

Legendary Lahore

About Lahore, there is a famous Punjabi saying, *Jineh Lahore nahi vekhya, o' jamya nahi* (Anyone who hasn't seen Lahore, is not yet born). Since I was born in Lahore, I was meant to return to this legendary city. My parents left Lahore when I was a year old, never to return.

The modern Royal Crown Plaza Hotel on the Upper Mall where I was staying is located beside the narrow canal that runs through the city, dividing the new from the old Lahore. My parents lived in Lahore from 1939 to 1942. Their modest terrace Barsati flat used to be on Nisbat Road. It is one of the main roads that takes you into the old city in the direction of the Red Fort and the Badshahi Mosque, through Gwala Mandi and Anarkali Bazaar. The three-storied buildings in that vicinity have the shops on the ground floor, a large flat on the first floor, and a smaller terrace flat on the top. During my parents' days in Lahore, the larger flat above the shop was occupied by one Butani family, and on the upper barsaati terrace lived the young Bhaneja couple, that is, my mother and father, until I arrived on the scene in

August 1941. The Bhanejas and Butanis continued their friendship over three generations, even when the families moved to India, settling in Delhi and Bombay (now Mumbai).

I had obtained my Lahore coordinates from one of the youngest of the Butani children in Mumbai who was twelve year old when I was brought home from the maternity hospital on Nisbat Road. There are many stories about the Nisbat Road home that have become folklore in our two families. How Sita Bhabhi, the matriarch of the Butani home, took my mother as a new bride under her wing, teaching her the basic skills of cooking and sewing, and even showing her how to put on the sari the way city women elegantly wrapped it around their petticoats. Despite a flight of stairs, the open courtyard in the two homes connected them for their daily chats.

Though Lahore is the second largest city in Pakistan, with a population of over ten million, finding Nisbat Road was not difficult. It is one of the old busy arteries of Lahore cutting north-south through the city and packed with dense traffic. Most buildings here from the 1930s are three to four stories high and reflect their age. Building No. 30 is quite close to the old Dayal Singh College.

On seeing me at the entrance checking the number on the building, the young owner of a real estate agency on the ground floor invited me inside. "Yes, this is 30 Nisbat Road. Who are you looking for?" I could only say: "My parents used to live in this building in the early 1940s."

When I explained to the young man that I was born in this building and that the two families called Bhaneja and Butani lived here as neighbours in the 1940s, the man looked baffled. "I am the fifth owner of the shop. There are no families left from pre-Partition days. Upstairs also people have changed and new floors have been added. Nothing is the same as before."

I inquired, "Would there be any way to see the upper floors?"

He shrugged his shoulders. "People upstairs would not like that. And then, again, you won't find anything from the time you are talking about."

He was reluctant to take me upstairs. You cannot just let in any man in a big city who stops at your doorstep. I was disappointed, but then I realized that there was not much in my memory about Lahore. There was no plaque or other memorabilia hidden in a wall that I could ask to look for. In the case of the ancestral locales of Upper Sindh, I had some vague recollections because of that one visit in 1946. It takes a child's memory more than a couple of years to accumulate impressions.

Responding to my recollections of the configurations of the flats lived in by the Bhanejas and the Butanis, the young man took me outside. He pointed to a well-kept building on the other side of the road. "Nisbat Road, I am told, used to have houses like that building in the old days." Unlike Number 30, which had changed considerably through additions, the other block still had the original layout—shops on the ground floor, two flats on the top, and a small barsaati flat on the terrace.

Since 30 Nisbat Road was a corner house, I stepped

into the side lane. The Butani twins had mentioned that they had great fun wheeling me in a pram in the side lane. I could only chuckle at the thought of the Butani youngsters now in their mid-seventies playing around with me in the pram.

My father used to joke with my mother about her cravings for kulfi ice cream during her last weeks of pregnancy while she carried me. He enjoyed telling us about taking her to Anarkali Bazaar for ice cream. A passerby directed me to Anarkali. The bazaar is one of the oldest markets of Lahore and named after a beautiful courtesan. The story goes that she was buried alive by the emperor Akbar as a punishment for having fallen in love with his son Jahangir. The old bazaar today is a labyrinth of lanes and alleys, with shops selling everything from antiques to clothing and jewellery. The Bano Bazaar is its "ladies-only" market. Finally, I did discover a glittery ice cream parlour called Gulshan Ice cream Shop. I wondered if it had been there in pre-Partition days. I recalled that one of my Punjabi family friends until my teenage years in Delhi used to call me Lahori. Only those born in Lahore are entitled to be called Lahori. My name Balwant is an unusual one for a Sindhi; it is in fact a pukka Lahori name.

From the bazaar to the famous Badshahi Mosque the ride on the autorickshaw was short. It dropped me in front of the tall new Minar-e-Pakistan monument built to commemorate the creation of Pakistan in August 1947. It is close to Badshahi Mosque and Red Fort. These two magnificent monuments in red stone and white marble dominate the old city. They were built in the sixteenth and seventeenth centuries during the Mogul reign, and are the precursors to similar buildings in Delhi and Agra.

Around sunset, standing at the latticed marble window of Moti Masjid (Pearl Mosque) in Red Fort, I caught a perspective of Badshahi Mosque. Next to it stands a gurudwara built by Maharaja Ranjit Singh (1780–1839), Punjab's prominent Sikh ruler. He was the same maharaja during whose reign the holy book of the Sikhs, Guru Granth Sahib, was carried on an elephant from Lahore for its installation in the newly built gurudwara in Hyderabad, Sindh. Ranjit Singh was the first Indian ruler in a thousand years to be able to thwart invaders from the northwest. History books are full of his valour and secular practices. Not only did he have a Muslim foreign minister in his court, he also banned the discriminatory zakat tax on Hindus and Sikhs imposed by the Mogul rulers.

The Ranjit Singh Samadhi Gurudwara in Lahore must have been in its full glory during pre-Partition days. The authors of *Freedom at Midnight* describe Lahore at that time as a tolerant city where communal distinctions between its 500,000 Hindus, 100,000 Sikhs, and 600,000 Muslims mattered less than anywhere else in India. (Collins and Lapierre p 237)

I thought of my parents on a tonga ride from Nisbat Road to the Red Fort, the mosque and the gurudwara. The coexistence of a gurudwara and a mosque on the same ground must have pumped my father's mystical tendencies—*Raste alug alug hain, thikana to ek hai* (the paths are different, the destination is the same) was one of his favourite Qawalis and used to be sung by his friends Shankar-Shambhu at the shrine of Sufi Khwaja Muinuddin Chishti in Ajmer. Despite being born Hindu, my father's spirit was essentially that of a Sufi whose belief rises above all castes, creeds, and faiths in search of universal love. As a seeker of wisdom and essentially a nonmaterialist, he combined in his temperament the two essentials from that tradition of Sufi dervishes. Once he wrote a letter to the editor of the *Ottawa Citizen* that ended with a Sufi alias of "Miskeen," which means a dervish, someone contented searching for higher love.

When my father's body was resting at the funeral parlour in Ottawa, awaiting cremation, an envelope arrived in the mail from Ajmer, India. It had been sent from the Chishti Dargah (shrine), and contained a short note from the convenor thanking my father for the donations he had been sending. Enclosed were dry rose petals from Chishti's Mazar. My younger brother passed on the envelope to me and we wondered what to do with the rose petals. The fragrance of the petals was still strong.

Daddy's body in his beige suit lay in the velvety cushioned coffin. The mortician had done a good job on his bespectacled face, bringing out his open optimistic smile. My mother, standing by the coffin, said, "O God, he looks alive." Then hesitantly she touched his palm as though not to disturb him in his sleep, bidding him her final goodbye. We decided to sprinkle the rose petals from the great Sufi's shrine around his body. In Lahore, this vignette from my memory got played out. Spirits have their own geography transcending all borders. They follow paths of love.

Facing me on the opposite side, I saw behind the onion shaped dome of Badshahi Mosque a big red sun slowly dropping down from an open crimson sky into the horizon. I was in bliss. In a way, my story was the same as that of my parents. This was a homecoming for both generations. Returning home is equivalent to restoring family honour in old societies. It makes the family proud of sons who went away, their return shows their humility, respect, and gratitude to the spirits who are already in heaven. My journey was completed. I felt as though the skin had gradually grown back on my bones which had for long been dry and brittle. I was glad I had chosen to travel this way. It brought closure to their (and my) longing for the homeland.

That night I made one last trip through Nisbat Road, to experience the new food streets that had emerged in 2000 in the old city in the Gwala Mandi, Anarkali, and Hira Mandi areas. The eateries, situated outside old haveli buildings, had the looks of traditional dhabas, with barbequing on open grills and tandoors. Parts of the streets were cordoned off from traffic and the side-street restaurants displayed their wares and dishes. They served the typical Lahori specialties of sheekh kebab, chicken tikka, thin and folded roomali roti, and chilled firnee served in earthen dishes. The chhajja balconies and roof tops of the buildings illuminated in blue and red lights, created an ambience of the Lahore of yesteryear.

Ironically, the city which in pre-Partition days had

shown such cultural diversity and tolerance, had at the creation of Pakistan became notorious for communal violence during those early days of nationhood. How could so much hate emanate from the very place where once goodwill and friendship had prevailed? I was in no position to pass judgement on the culture of post-Independence Lahore. The inclusive humanist ethos of my father originated in this part of the Indian subcontinent. I was glad to be part of that heritage.

The next morning was my last in Pakistan. The road to Lahore airport from the Upper Mall was in the opposite direction to the old city. South Lahore was full of large kothi bungalows, one topping the other in design and construction. Near these large houses were modern shopping centres, stylish restaurants, and beautifully designed hotels, different from what I saw yesterday in the old city. The centre of gravity of the city seemed to have shifted to the south, to the prosperous civil lines and military cantonment, evidently benefitting from the riches of the country's military elite.

Just as we were approaching the airport, I noticed in the bright morning sunshine a row of cricket pitches with young men in shining white trousers, shirts, and pullovers net-practicing. What surprised me this spring morning was the large number of pitches, a reminder of the common craze for the game on both sides of the border. Some of the Pakistani cricketers, such as Hanif Mohammad, Imran Khan, and Wasim Akram, whom I admired as the world's best, must have practiced at similar nets across the country.

I was back at the Allama Iqbal International Airport

for my noon flight to Delhi. It was here a week ago that I had begun my odyssey into a new and an old land—the land of my ancestors, the land of my birth, then British India, now Pakistan. It was time to say goodbye.

13

The "Refugee" Prime Minister: Dr I K Gujral

The Gandhian way teaches us about value of diversity and respect for human beings. Gandhi never wanted a cult to develop around him.

Back in India, my final meeting before leaving the subcontinent for Canada was with the former prime minister Dr Inder Kumar Gujral in New Delhi. Dr Gujral, an octogenarian, had one of the most interesting backgrounds among Indian politicians. He had lived an active life as a scholar, social activist, and senior civil servant, as well as a politician who had served on both sides in the Indian Parliament. He had been the leader of the world's largest democracy. For me, an additional interesting aspect in his background was that he was born in Pakistan in a small town near Lahore before migrating to India with his family after the Partition. His term as India's prime minister in 1997–1998, though brief, was a remarkable one because of the steps taken during that period towards rapprochement with Pakistan.

Dr Gujral's official residence, a large colonial bungalow surrounded by a leafy garden, was on 5 Janpath. We met in his office-cum-sitting room. A snow-white goatee with silvery sideburns and receding hairline marked his long face. It is rather unusual to see an Indian politician with a goatee. He reminded me of a French savant from the 1960s. Looking distinguished in his steel grey safari suit, he had wiry spectacles with large lenses sitting on his thin nose. His relaxed manner put me at ease. Taking a chair by his desk, he smiled and invited me and my cousin to sit on the sofa in front. Two abstract paintings hung on two walls in the office. I recognized one, by his brother Satish Gujral, the famous Indian architect and painter.

Dr Gujral mentioned his special relationship with Lahore. Only two years ago he had been invited to Pakistan as the special guest of honour at a function and was awarded an honorary degree at his old alma mater, Punjab University in Lahore. He had studied in Punjab's capital for eight years. Described as India's most educated PM, he had three doctoral degrees, one of them earned while he was in Lahore in the 1940s. I told him briefly of the places I had visited during my travels.

The meeting was a courtesy call I was making on behalf of an American friend, Glenn D Paige of Hawaii. Paige had recently written a book, *Nonkilling Global Political Science* (2002), which Dr Gujral upon reading had remarked must be taught in every university political science department. The book takes the perspective that human killing is a problem that should be solved rather than accepted as a condition that must be endured forever.

In Pakistan it appeared that not much effort had been made to create a space for nonviolent peace and human rights. We could only identify the late Khan Abdul Gaffar Khan as the exception. But then Abdul Gaffar Khan had spent most of his life in Pakistani prisons, much longer than he had spent in a British prison for the struggle for independence. He was branded as unpatriotic for being a faithful follower of Mahatma Gandhi and for his unflinching belief that Islam was a nonviolent and peaceful religion.

I asked Dr Gujral what he thought about the place and relevance of Mahatma Gandhi on the entire subcontinent in the twenty-first century. He was reluctant to comment on the situation on the subcontinent, but replied that as far as India was concerned, "Gandhian heritage is now beyond Mahatma's statues, museums, and exhibitions. It has now become part of our psyche. The way political conflicts are resolved today in India can be generally described as the Gandhian way—the nonviolent democratic way."

He told me the story of his beginnings as a member of parliament.

"In my first speech to the House, as Prime Minister, I began with the words 'I am a refugee.' I said that I was surprised that a refugee had been chosen to be a prime minister. I had come here without a penny, starting in this country like many refugees, empty-handed on a railway platform. Eventually, I made my life through hard work to where I am."

It seemed his personal story had relevance to our conversation. He believed that support for pluralism and democratic governance in India was connected with Mahatma Gandhi.

"My parents were nonpolitical. They both went to jail during the freedom struggle. My mother went overnight, as they say, 'from veil to jail.' My lawyer father put on homespun khadi clothes to join Gandhiji. Friends began asking him why he was giving up all for a half-naked fakir, a crank who wants to take on the British Empire for a fistful of salt . . . Gandhiji's search for Truth, in which we all joined him, demanded discernment, tolerance, respect for diversity while aspiring for unity. It was not just national unity but a plea for the unity of spirit that cut across race, religion, and gender."

Looking for an illustration of the Gandhian ethos in the public psyche, he remembered a recent incident in the Lok Sabha, the Indian Parliament. "Advani-ji (the Opposition Bharatiya Janata Party leader, who was born in Sindh) in a parliamentary debate recently was heckled by another MP, who called him a refugee. That created a furor in the house, almost all the members of the House were asking the MP to apologize for his inappropriate language. Those MPs who were seeking an apology were not from Advani-ji's own party, but from other parties. That's Gandhian."

He continued: "Gandhi-ji fought superstition and always looked for a rational solution. His experiments with himself and with others were open-ended, trying to find truth and then to seek nonviolent means to resolve that issue. The Gandhian way teaches us about the value of diversity and respect for human beings. Gandhi never wanted a cult to develop around him."

I wanted him to elaborate on his comment about a cult as I thought he was implying that on the other side of the border politics had degenerated into dogmatism. He carefully studied me for a moment, wondering how far he should go with his explaining. "Let's go back to the time of the creation of India and Pakistan. Mr Jinnah on his first visit to Dhaka in 1948 defined Pakistan to be 'One Nation, One Religion, and One Language,' that one language as we all know was Urdu. That was the day the seeds for a separate Bangladesh were sown in East Pakistan." The statement had been made very calmly. Checking whether I was paying attention, he added, "Now look at India around the same time. The most secessionist state in India at that time was Tamil-speaking in the south. Its leaders felt that once Hindi would become the national language, the country would be dominated and absorbed by the north. In Parliament, when an MP from the south raised the idea of Tamil as the national language, Prime Minister Nehru replied 'why Tamil only, it should be English, Hindi, and Tamil.' Ultimately fourteen languages became the officially recognized languages. That sort of flexibility, adjustment, consensus-building are part of India's Gandhian tradition of mutual respect and accommodation."

Today, the number of officially recognized languages is twenty-two.

Dr Gujral's comment reminded me of the Sindhi nationalists who had in the past declared Pakistan Central government's approaches to national integration as "imposed homogeneity." He came back with another illustration of pluralism in action in India, that of the

Hindu-Muslim riots that took place in Godhra a couple of years ago. "The Gujarat riots shamed Indians. The commission, headed by an independent justice, looked at the matter to find out the truth. The conclusions identified the culprits and cleared the air. The two communities realized that it was something between brothers in a family. Muslims are an integral part of India, and equal partners in the Indian experiment in all fields of life."

I noticed the words "Indian experiment in all fields of life." Gandhi had used the same language. Gujral continued with the theme of communal harmony in India. "It may often take long to see results, to correct distrust after a communal riot, but the Indian way is to seek political resolution. Gandhi wanted a consensus-based democracy, as that was the nonviolent way to practice politics. Gandhi opted for parliamentary democracy as the next best because democracy means essentially finding (nonviolent) ways to bring peace in politics."

When Gujral became Prime Minister in 1997, people to people contact between India and Pakistan was among his first initiatives. That year marked the beginning of the exchanges of delegations of writers, journalists, and artists between the two countries. The trend over the past decade has continued with similar exchanges led by businessmen, politicians, and even sports personalities, mainly the national cricket teams from both sides playing on Indian and Pakistani grounds.

As Dr Gujral walked us towards the portico of his official residence to say goodbye, I thought it was a perfect way to cap my roots journey, calling on this most educated refugee prime minister of India.

Epilogue

Love is an emotion to be acted upon. This trip to my ancestral land was an effort to transform the emotions of belongingness that had bristled within me into something tangible. The visit to the homeland of my parents had brought a sense of fulfilment and a closure, giving me a better understanding of myself and of the human bond which, despite the Partition, united the people across the border.

Birla House on Tees January Marg is just a few blocks away from Dr Gujral's residence. A visit to Birla House at the start of my journey to Pakistan two weeks ago had brought to mind Mahatma Gandhi's favourite hymn, *Vaishnav jan to tene kahiye . . .*" He is a true devotee of God who identifies himself with others' sorrows and while so doing has no pride about himself."

Gandhi remained most of his life a misunderstood person. In India he was vilified by those whose families had lost members to Muslim marauders on the other side of the border. Extremist Hindus saw him as an appeaser of Muslims and other minorities. They blamed him for his inability to prevent Partition. In Pakistan, he was described as the mortal enemy of the new nation, who never wanted the creation of Pakistan. But Gandhi's opposition to Partition had more to do with the fear of a bloodbath. Instead of revelling in the creation of the two new nations, he was concerned with the deep-seated problems of the caste system, communal sectarianism, and dire poverty, which lay behind the acts of gruesome violence across the subcontinent. In Pakistan, Gandhi's fasts and his visits to areas of violence in order to protect Muslims were overlooked. For Mahatma Gandhi there was no "other," all were sparks of the same Divine, children of the same God.

Standing at the large round circle from where emerges Tees January Marg, I was reminded of how I held on to my father as a six-year-old in the lawn of Birla House where Gandhi had every evening held his inter-denominational prayers. It was the simplicity of that powerful message of one universal God and the unity of faiths that upset many. This trip had also made me realize how difficult it was in the post 9/11 security environment to shake off national and religious prejudices, irrespective of which side of the border one stood on. My brief encounter with Muslim youths on the train journey to Lahore was a good example of my trepidation in the new security environment and the shallowness of my secular convictions when put to test.

Self-imposed or self-chosen exile is a universal phenomenon, even Gandhi chose to leave India twice in his lifetime—to England for studies, and to South Africa to earn a living. Journeys, whether undertaken by individuals or nations, cannot be fathomed from start to finish; however, our values often shape the directions of those journeys. Hindu Sindhis who chose to leave their native land became one of the most cosmopolitan people of India, adopting the whole of India as their own, and many left India to settle abroad as successful traders and businessmen.

Why we decide to leave our homelands is not easy to figure out—why we left five minutes earlier, when leaving five minutes later would have completely changed the course of our fate. We must ultimately face the consequence for the choice we make, whether it arises from the partitioning of a country, abandoning one's homeland for fear of persecution, or migrating to a distant land for economic reasons . . . or even returning home for a glimpse of one's roots. I recall a moment at my father's funeral at the crematorium in Ottawa. As the eldest son I had to push the red knob on the furnace in which the body of my father lay in the velvet coffin, awaiting cremation. The furnace was hidden in the basement, away from the congregation. I loathed to press the button, for I know my father would have liked to be cremated under a clear blue sky on a pyre of burning logs in the open ground. There was a hurt inside me, difficult to express. In Hindu tradition, the eldest son, clad in the mourning attire of white pyjama and kurta, kindles the pyre on which the body of the deceased parent draped in white cotton rests. Now, dressed in a western black suit for the occasion, I cringed as I pushed the red button. I saw the flicker of a flame in the steel entrapment through a tiny glass window. It was all over. That is the price one pays for choosing to dislocate oneself.

My fractured identity sometimes confuses, sometimes pleases me; eventually I know the question of belonging will in its own time sort itself out. Home now is no longer just one place, but all those places where my wife and I have been and are—places of our ancestors, our own, and our children's, and various other places we travelled to and felt connected to . . . where you can smell the earth, the air, the water, and marvel at what unites these elements and us. One of my friends, Mark Frutkin, in his recent book, *Erratic North: A Vietnam Draft Resistor's Life in the Canadian Bush,* describes his identity as "Catholic-Jewish-soon-to-be-Buddhist-German-Russian-Irish-English-French." He is not atypical in the North American context. He writes that land is just one element in a fluid interconnected world; the added overlays of cultures in which a refugee and immigrant lives and grows up are equally significant.

Standing in the airy spacious part of New Delhi in front of Birla House, I thought about those of us who have lived most of our lives on the move, with many overlays of cultures and places. How does identity play out for us, can an individual from one place ever become part of another place in time? I was not thinking of my parents or my refugee relatives, but this time about my wife and I, who are from two very different cultures and immigrated to a country called Canada, a new nation that was struggling to find its own notion of national identity.

It was time to head back to that home now—a land which, unlike Upper Sindh, remained for most of the winter frozen, covered by snow yet alive underneath.

Select Bibliography

Ashe, Geoffrey. (1968, 2000). *Gandhi—A Biography*. New York: Cooper Square Press.

Collins, Larry and Dominique Lapierre. (1997). *Freedom at Midnight*. New Delhi :Vikas Publishing House Pvt. Ltd.

Frutkin, Mark. (2008). *Erratic North: A Vietnam Draft Resister's Life in the Canadian Bush*. Toronto: Dundurn Press.

Gandhi, Rajmohan. (2007, 2008). *Biography—The Man, His People, and the Empire*. Berkeley: University of California Press.

Malkani, K R. (1984). *The Sindh Story*. New Delhi: Allied Publishers.

Paige, Glenn D. (2002, 2009). *Nonkilling Global Political Science*. Philadelphia: Xlibris.

Wolpert, Stanley. (1984, 2005). *Jinnah of Pakstan*. New Delhi: Oxford UP.

Acknowledgements

My sincere thanks to the following: M G Vassanji, for his thorough and careful editing of my manuscript, TSAR publisher Nurjehan Aziz, and Rahul Varma for introducing me to TSAR. Gratitude to Mark Frutkin, Glenn Paige, Adrian de Hoog, and Paul Thompson for reading earlier drafts. My deep gratitude to Terence McNamee who in his review of the manuscript challenged me to look at my "Canadianese" (his word) and saw an interesting connection between my personal life story and the journey in this book. Anita Rizvi, who like me has ancestral connections in India and Pakistan, and confirmed the universal humanist values woven in the book's narrative. Profound thanks to her and also to friend and former colleague Stuart Hughes. Without Stuart's hosting in Islamabad, this journey would never have taken place. I am doubly grateful to him as Editor of the *Bout de Papier,* the journal of Canadian foreign service officers, for having chosen to publish excerpts in the Bout. In life's journeys, our paths cross with individuals who provide unexpected moments which form the grist for a travel memoir. I am grateful to all of them—from a hospitable family in my father's old neighbourhood, to a taxi driver, a "refugee" Prime Minister, and many others. Thanks to my sons Neil and Raoul for inspiring me to reflect on the meaning of our identity in a globalizing world, and most importantly to my most patient and understanding wife, Marie Gaffney Bhaneja, without whose support and encouragement this journey would not have taken place.

Permissions Credits

Permission obtained from the copyright holders for the material referenced in this work:

Erratic North (2008) by Mark Frutkin, Dundurn Press, 3 Church St. Suite 500, Toronto, ON M5E 1M2, permission from the author.

Freedom at Midnight (1975) by Larry Collins and Dominique Lapierre, Simon and Shuster, permission from Renaissance Literary & Talent, Post Office Box 17379, Beverly Hills, California 90209. USA.

Gandhi: A Biography by Geoffrey Ashe(2000), First Cooper Square Press, permission from The Rowman & Littlefield Publishing Group, 4501 Forbes Blvd, Suite 200, Lanham, Maryland 20706. USA.

Every effort has been made to obtain permission from all copyright holders whose material is included in this book but in some cases this has not proved possible at the time of going to press. I wish to thank those copyright holders who responded and are gratefully acknowledged above. At the same time, I wish to thank those who are included without acknowledgement, I would be pleased to rectify any omissions in future editions.

Other works by Balwant Bhaneja:

Quest for Gandhi: A Nonkilling Journey

Two Plays by Vijay Tendulkar: The Cyclist and His Fifth Woman (in collaboration with Vijay Tendulkar)

Science and Government: The Nehru Era

Afghanistan: Political Modernization of a Mountain Kingdom

The Politics of Triangles: A Study in South Asian International Relations

Balwant Bhaneja was born in Lahore and left India in 1965 for Canada. He has written widely on politics, science, and the arts. His two recent books include a collaboration with Indian playwright Vijay Tendulkar as a translator and adaptor of a book of drama, entitled: *Two Plays: The Cyclist* and *His Fifth Woman* (2006) published by Oxford University Press (India), and a creative nonfiction work, *Quest for Gandhi: A Nonkilling Journey* (2010) by Center for Global Nonkilling, Honolulu, USA and IGINP-CESCI, Madurai, India. His plays have been produced by BBC World Service, Ottawa's Odyssey Theatre, and Toronto's Maya Theatre at Harbourfront. Currently, he is working on a drama adaptation of the award-winning novel *Fabrizio's Return* by Mark Frutkin. A former Canadian diplomat, he holds a PhD from the University of Manchester.